COUNTING THE COUNT IN BUSINESS CONSULTING

IDEATION OF TOP 40 BUSINESS CONSULTANTS

COUNTING THE COUNT IN BUSINESS CONSULTING

IDEATION OF TOP 40 BUSINESS CONSULTANTS

Dr. Enoch O. Antwi

Counting The Count In Business Consulting:
Ideation of Top 40 Business Consultants
Copyright © 2019 by Dr. Enoch O. Antwi

All rights reserved. No part of this publication may be reproduced, distributed, or transmitted in any form or by any means, including photocopying, recording, or other electronic or mechanical methods, without the prior written permission of the publisher or author, except in the case of brief quotations embodied in critical reviews and certain other noncommercial uses permitted by copyright law.

Although every precaution has been taken to verify the accuracy of the information contained herein, the author and publisher assume no responsibility for any errors or omissions. No liability is assumed for damages that may result from the use of information contained within.

Library of Congress Control Number: *2019916432*
ISBN-13:   Paperback: *978-1-950073-87-0*

Printed in the United States of America

GoToPublish LLC
1-888-337-1724
www.gotopublish.com
info@gotopublish.com

CONTENTS

GRATITUDE ix
Preface xi
Introduction xiii

Ideation I   How Do Consultants Set Their Fees? 1
Ideation II   Do Leaders have Plans of
              Opportunities for Employees? 6
Ideation III Diversity:
              Motivating Women to Achieve Success
              in Consulting 10
Ideation IV   Customer Service:
              How Consultants Spend Time on a
              given Assignment. 15
Ideation V   Coaching:
              Biggest Risk of Managers Today 19
Ideation VI   How to Unravel Problems during Consulting 23
Ideation VII How Do Students Enter into the Consulting Field? . 26
Ideation VIII The Future of Consulting is the
              Knowledge of Change 30

Ideation IX	Marketing in its Real Sense	33
Ideation X	Consultants are like Actors on a Stage	37
Ideation XI	The 39th Consultant: Insights from the Class	40

Final Ideations

- Sitting Home Alone: Leadership is Key. 44
- Learning Agility – Leading Towards Your Best. 58
- Interviewing Skills 64
- The Steward Leader... 87
- The Servant as Leader.. 92
- Power in Leadership 95
- Measuring Leadership Performance Through Coaching .. 99
- A New View of Life and Work for Leaders....................... 102
- Judgment on the Job 115
- International Negotiations.. 128
- Writing Grant: For Non-profits... 139
- Take AIM in Conflict Resolution...................................... 144
- Business Case for Diversity and Inclusion (D&I)............ 152
- Business Case for Diversity & Inclusion: A Chamber of Commerce Commitment..................... 174
- Final Ideation: My Message to You. 182

References 196

To my family, friends and work colleagues.

May you always treasure love and understanding.

GRATITUDE

THE AUTHOR STARTED consulting with the German Technical/Financial Cooperation in 2002. However, most of the ideation of this practical book was originally compiled in graduate school class discussions, presentations, seminars, committee meetings and concepts in some publications during the past decade. A personal journal and research of this compilation chronicles different consultants' worldview, which has been coherently weaved into a simple book for business consultants. I have revised some of the thoughts in paraphrases; most of them substantially, while others have been quoted directly for the purposes of emphasis. The various chapters are titled "Ideations" because ideation is the creative process of generating, developing, and communicating new ideas through innovation, development and actualization in the field of business consulting.

Special gratitude goes to Professor George Manning, whose business consulting class produced 38 top consultants' ideations. They shared their personal and professional experience, worthy for other consultants to know. The two remaining consultants, to make the number 40, is George himself and the author of this book. My aim has been to create a real consulting book with diverse practical stories, a coherent exploration of the consulting profession that engages divergent outlooks for the better of business.

There were other professors in leadership and business courses who are consultants and colleagues. They shared their experiences and stories as well. I mentioned the provenance of this book foundation partly because I believe in truth in labeling, and partly because the individuals who shared knowledge, with all the trust that implies, are valued partners in my own ideas and in the consulting profession.

Other chapters such as learning agility was originally shared by a consulting colleague. Interviewing skills and Steward Leadership were ideas at lectures and conferences. The exceptional discussions that accompanied the lectureship and conferences helped frame this portion of the book. The remaining chapters were based on research, personal consulting and lectures the author have conducted for businesses and students and feedbacks.

Much of the personal journey embedded in personal ideation of the book was made in the company of, and with the support of family and work colleagues, past and present. Special thanks also go to Emma Davies, my publisher's Fulfillment Officer and Mae Carbona, the publishing consultant who made the first cold call. I did not mention individual work-colleagues in my gratitude narrative simply because their story belongs to them alone. Thank you all for the love and passion you have given me along the way.

PREFACE

BUSINESS CONSULTANTS PLAY significant roles in making organizations achieve high positive outcomes. My interest in writing this book started from the summer of 2009, when I took an eight-week intensive graduate course in Organizational Consulting. As an international leadership consultant and a doctoral student at that time, I had great passion for the course. I learned a lot from my fellow students and the thirty-eight (38) invited consultants. The course had an expectation of students reading and discussing a *text* on contemporary consulting issues and a *reader* on consulting as a calling. There were also panel presentations and insights from practitioners, gate keepers, and buyers of consulting services. This book chronicles my journal experience in that course and a personal reflection.

Book Organization.

The book begins with an Introduction of the need for consulting. Then, there are ten ideations and shared best practices of 38 top-level business consultants in each session. Each session's main topic and best practices are recounted with each consultant's name and ideas shared. The goal was to cite sources, just as reviewing literature on the topic. The eleventh ideation is from the professor who organized the course.

The final reflection is from the author's academic and professional consulting experience. Related topics discussed include: Leadership is Key - Trust and Mistrust for Leaders; Learning Agility, Interviewing Skills, The Steward Leader (with a piece of Servant Leadership), Power in Leadership, Measuring Leadership Performance through Coaching, A New View of Life and Work of Leaders, Judgment on the Job, International Negotiations, Writing Grants – For Nonprofits, Take AIM in Conflict Resolution, Business Case for Diversity & Inclusion, and Final Reflective Thoughts. Notably, there are Exercises for each Ideation or chapter to determine competencies in learning.

The book is a textbook as well as a *guidebook* for business consultants and lecturers. The ideation reflects on panel discussions and presentations, which were conducted in a plenary session in the field of consulting, training, and executive coaching. Each ideation is based on a particular class discussion while the final ideations is a sum of emerged themes based on insights from each class reflection as well as professional experience of the author. The book could serve as professional and educational guide for consultants, trainers, executive coaches, facilitators, leaders, managers, college professors, prospective consultants, and students who want to enter into the consulting business.

INTRODUCTION

*Not everything that can be counted counts;
not everything that counts can be counted.*
—Albert Einstein

THE ULTIMATE GOAL of consulting is knowledge sharing and awareness creation. Consultants, trainers, and executive coaches have an ultimate purpose for what they do: helping organizations in decision-making and project improvements; finding answers within a group of employees by asking appropriate questions, contributing to knowledge in the field of consulting, understanding what organizations do, and learning in the process through inquiries and evaluations.

Learning from each consulting assignment is an important process because organizations could be complex and differs in many aspects. People in organizations differ from one another, management styles differ, stakeholders differ, and questions that guide inquiries also differ. Data that seek to elucidate inquiry questions like mini-surveys, interviews, observations, documents, and experiments also differs in every situation and from individual consultant, trainer or coach to the other. Evidently, there are vast differences in issues and instances that guide consultants' exploration as they help organizations find solutions to challenges, issues, and problems. Most consultants use theory-derived, theory-testing, or theory-oriented questionnaires and surveys to find answers. Others use practical, applied, or action-oriented questions. Yet, others observe, watch from a distance, and come out with solutions.

In all situations that consultants consult for, some issues may be of personal interest and concern while others may not. Many consultants consult on areas or subjects with little interest, passion, or no practical training while others develop interest and passion through hands-on training. Evidently, experiences gained from years of working or on various fields of endeavors could help a consultant meet and surmount all the challenges of her job. At the end of the day, consultants heavily rely on knowledge, experience and resources to help seek answers (the why?) for organizations.

Caution! Consultants should not be consulting for financial gains, but building deeper-relations with managers and employees in organizations.

Obviously, building relations in troubled organizations could be a tricky business because it appears every organization has its own criteria of judging quality of a consultant's work and how they build relations. Fundamentally, it is easier to dance to the music of management or leadership because they hire and pay for consulting services. However, ethics and posterity call for sound judgment and fairness in consulting. Research and experience have shown that consulting is like many people dancing to a heart-touching music of inviting melody. They could spin, twirl, wag, wiggle, wave, shake, squat, sit, summersault, buggy, twist, or flip together, but might not hear the same beat or rhythm of that single source of music.

Consulting ideas could also be placed in relevant context based on the knowledge and experience of the consultant and prior investigation of the organization one is to consult for. This gives the consultant a clear understanding of the strengths and weaknesses of the organization (a simple SWOT analysis). It also guides the consultant to meet recruiters' expectations. Noticeably, groups, be it employees, followers, associations, unions, or teams experience differences in opinions, thoughts, and styles of leadership. **The popular saying that we can always agree to disagree agreeably is true**. Perhaps, these differences in thought-process are the keystone of every consultant's present challenges in organizations in an effort to get a common ground of business operations for effective outcome.

There is wisdom in diversity of information and ideas at the workplace. It is the consultant's responsibility to provide that strategic diversified information to ensure that expected organizational results are attained. **Not every leader or employee would accept the consultant's recommendations**. Some may fight it while others will embrace it. Sometimes, management accepts the consultant's findings while employees reject it. The opposite is true in some situations. Whatever the case may be, it takes at least, two, to tango. The consultant should be able to invite both parties (leaders and employees) to the dancing floor for dialogue and agreed to common solutions so that at least, there could be similar themes in the ears of all parties dancing to the theme of the same music. After all, the consultant, management and employees are all trying to open the right doors with the right keys in solving a pertinent or recurring problem.

It seems logical to state that consultant's honest attempt to understand unfair organizational practices, policies behind those practices, and previous attempts by management in resolving those touchy practices may be the first step of getting to the core of organizational challenges. However, vagueness of information usually supplied by managers who hire consultants abound in most organizations, which makes it difficult for consultants to dig the truth from the heart of organizational problems.

A consultant may spend weeks, months, or years on a given organization's assignment trying to fix the problem, sometimes to the detriment of his/her family and relations. The least said about the constant travels, risks, and physical absence from home, the better. Bottom line: Is a particular individual, group, system, design, culture, or policy the heart of a controversy in an organization that calls for a special attention? What do the employees want? What does management want? What do stakeholders want? What appropriate, timely and relevant questions are asked? What relevant answers are given? Do the questions spark argument or development? **And, do they count when it needs to be counted for the organization's success? To get answers, let's count the count from different consultants' perspective.** Note that all ideations from other consultants are written in present terms to make the story come alive. Some might have retired or moved on now. The author used only their first names with intent.

IDEATION I

(With Tom, Peter, Terri, and Linda)

How Do Consultants Set Their Fees?

TOM IS THE director of Keating and Associates, a consortium in Kentucky, USA. He talked about trends in business consulting in a plenary session. Tom has a background in different field of careers. Currently, he practices as an external management consultant. Tom opened the discussion with an assertion that every organization, business, and institution needs a consultant. His vision is a passion of seeing people developing to exceed their expectations, and believes multi-tasking should be a hallmark of a good consultant. Peter, on the other hand, have spent 35 years in the hospitality industry as a consultant. He has passion for opening franchises in his travels around the world. Unlike Tom, Peter has stayed in the hospitality business all his life. **Peter's secret is that he enjoys his work, and learns from it everyday.**

Linda, a business consultant started consulting in Japan. She has worked as tax accountant for many U.S law and manufacturing firms. Currently, she is a Human Resources director in the U.S state court for six years and practices as an external consultant. She has passion for business successes and like Tom, **has accumulated consulting expertise and skills from different careers.** Terri is the president of *Just the Basics, Inc*, a national non-profit and social agency consulting. Terri is a mother, wife, and an external consultant. She has worked with a number of companies, and learned on the job. According to Terri, she has learned to balance her work with family responsibilities. She learns more than what she shares as a consultant.

The panel discussions centered on the role of a consultant. The panelists agreed that **consultants should be the catalyst for leaders of businesses and organizations' problem –solving and development.** It was clear that expertise and open-mindedness were important for successful consulting. For instance, without adequate knowledge in a specific area, one may not excel in that area of consulting. Open-mindedness also allows consultants to listen to the challenges of an organization to know their pressing needs. Arguably, the solution lies in the organization, not the consultant. Peter specifically posited that a consultant needs to do much research into an area she wants to consult; know who she is working for, and the timeline for accomplishing set goals.

Setting consulting fees was one of the major questions on the floor. The panelists conceptualized that **it is better for a consultant to know his/her value before charging a fee**. The panelists also agreed that the fee depended on an area one consults for, the consultant's operating cost, and start-up cost. Their advice was that, a consultant should be dynamic and versatile. She should be ready to learn new things, and develop herself in other areas of consulting.

The bottom line, said the panelists, was to ask oneself, what does success looks like? This should be one's objective in consulting. Thereafter, the consultant should adapt to the clients' plan, ask diagnostic questions, and facilitate in every consulting program or event.

Other issues discussed were the integration of other departments into performance management. For instance, a stagnant growth in the marketing department should encompass not only a comprehensive marketing plan with a competent sale manger, but also management ensuring that research and development department adheres to quality control standards and quality responses. All departments should also be part of the strategic planning implementation both in the short, medium, and the long-term.

Further discussions centered on succession planning as an important factor to consider in a business as a going concern so that trust, continuity, growth, and expansion could occur. As an example, basic financial details of cash flow, profit and loss account, and balance sheet should not be left to few top management and middle management alone. Each employee should be able to access financial information to know what is going on and take ownership of being important part of the outcome.

Herein rests the hard logic: If employees do not know how the company earns and spends money and resources or the profit and loss the employees themselves have contributed, management cannot expect the employees to be more motivated to contribute to the future success of the organization. **There is also the tendency of gossips, speculations and negative perceptions in organizations when financial information is blocked or filtered to employees.**

Talking to employees and looking at the pattern of events from existing data, observations or interviews could guide the consultant to enhance a collegial culture, help build trust, and improve mentoring for effective succession planning. The caution is that, square pegs should not be in round holes in the succession planning process. The discussion continued on how to build trusting relationship at the workplace. One of the students said there is too much mistrust in organizations. Another said **mistrust comes as much from what employees don't know as from what they do know**. Management should be open, fair, share their feelings, fears and expectations with all employees; tell the truth, show consistency, fulfill their promises, and maintain confidence. If these worthwhile attributes are lacking in management, employees would not perceive them as trustworthy and trust will be an elusive concept.

Exercises:

a. Discuss ways consultants could help organization's decision-making and project improvements. Do you think the answers are in the organization or with the consultant? Support your response with relevant examples.
b. Discuss some of the appropriate questions a consultant may ask in getting solutions to organizational problems.
c. "Organizational conflicts stem from unfair practices and policies." Write a three- page reflection paper to agree or disagree with this statement citing experienced or witnessed examples.
d. Some managers supply vague information to consultants, which makes it difficult to dig the truth from the heart of the organizational problems. Do you agree or disagree with the statement? Explain.
e. Is the consulting time spent on travels, risks and physical absence from home worth it salt? Why or why not?
f. Most of the time, an individual, group, system, design or culture spark controversies in organizations and consultants may be needed to resolve the conflict. Where would you begin in resolving a conflict if the statement above is true?
g. Is it necessary to know one's value before charging for a consulting fee? How do we quantify a consultant's value in costing terms?

h. In your opinion, what are the most efficient ways consultants could help organizations improve quality and diversity interventions?
i. Do consultants need to specialize in passion areas or develop themselves in other areas of consulting? Explain.

IDEATION II

(With Gordon, Connie, Wagner, Rob, & Amy)

Do Leaders have Plans of Opportunities for Employees?

GORDON IS THE founder of Duke and Associates, a consulting firm in Kentucky, USA, and a former Secretary of Finance, Commonwealth of Kentucky. Gordon gained numerous experiences from different works to build his expertise level before entering into consulting. He concentrates on only two major Fortune 500 primary clients. Connie is the vice president, Human Resource Development, of a major insurance Western & Southern Insurance Company in Cincinnati, Ohio. Both consultants have changed many careers before entering into consulting.

John, vice president of Kroger retail stores in Greater Cincinnati is in charge of over 275,000 US employees under unionized organizations. John has worked to revamp 16 major pension plans for clients who were all under water, and has been working for 31years, eleven of those years in consulting. He prides himself of holding different positions and responsibilities in his career, and has helped Kroger retail store improved quality and diversity interventions. Rob is the executive director, Metropolitan Education and Training Services (METS), Northern Kentucky, USA. Rob is also an international consultant for utility companies, and external consultant for Kroger projects. He is an instructor who has taught in many universities, and now combines consulting with teaching. He specializes in conflict resolution and fair employment practice laws. Rob admits to having done a bit of everything in his career and learned from his mistakes. Amy is the director of organizational effectiveness, Cincinnati Children's Hospital Medical Center. Amy worked with Cinergy (a utility firm) for seven years before moving to Cincinnati Children Hospital in Ohio, USA. Culture is a huge thing for her, and she loves to build systems bottom-up. She currently runs executive assessments and build sustainable processes at Cincinnati Children Hospital.

This plenary discussion centered on many components of consulting. The first was action-learning opportunities. Panelists and students (learning associates) agreed that **leadership should develop plans to make sure their employees get opportunities for learning and growth**. For instance, lack of opportunities leads to lack of motivation to work. The multi-million question in many organizations is: Do employees believe that if they give a maximum effort it will be reflected in their performance appraisals? Most performance appraisals are merit-based. That means salary adjustments and promotions are based on such appraisal results.

If the organization's performance appraisal system is designed to access factors such as allegiance, flexibility, or bravery, more effort in getting the job done may not necessarily lead to higher performance appraisal results because such words could be subjective and dictated by managers or supervisors. There is also the possibility of an employee being disliked by the manager, supervisor, or immediate team leader for no concrete reason except personality crush and petty personal feelings that might not have anything to do with the job. As a result, the employee will expect low opportunities or deprived appraisal results regardless of her level of effort. *Management has ethical responsibility not to reward their favorites. Consultants have moral obligation to echo that point.*

Naturally, some managers never condemn their own ideas and think it should stand "as is," or with little modification. That is wrong and they should be told in the face even if it means such managers will not hire the consultant's services again. One sensitive issue on the floor of discussion was a question of receiving appropriate opportunities acceptable to the employee. Do the twenty-five cents pay raise get appreciated by employees? Could management think of more creative ways of rewarding employees with higher inputs? What form should the rewards take? Do the "thank you" and gift cards work? How do management tailor rewards to individual employee needs? One way is for management to consult the employee in the assessment process so that the rewards could perfectly fit employee needs. Certainly, if a manager provides a reward and the employee has no relevant use of it, the reward becomes a waste of resources, time, and energy of the manager, employee and the organization. Unfortunately, most managers claim they are limited in the amount of rewards they can provide thus, making it difficult for them to individualize rewards. The panelists suggested that managers could strengthen relationships between employees' efforts and performances by seeking their input in the process. This process is an art, not a science. Common sense could be applied to meet individual needs.

Finally, the issue of talent management in organizations was brought to the fore. The panelists submitted that a top or middle-level manager should be in charge of talent management in every organization. The person could be called "Talent Manager" or any exotic name management may choose. Personally, I would want to link succession planning with talent development as a core function of the "Talent Manager" because both situations identify suitable internal candidates through mentoring, training, and job rotation to replace key players in the organization as needed.

The process begins with management realizing that the employees are the most valuable assets. Therefore, management should place priority on developing its employees and include them in the organization's processes to attract competent, committed, and diligent employees.

Exercises

a. Could there be wrong rewards in organizations? If so, how do such rewards affect time, energy and resources of management, employees and the organization?
b. Do modern organizations need talent managers? How could they function effectively without duplicating other management functions?
c. Which of these are the most valuable assets of organizations: Management or employee? Explain your answer with examples.
d. In what ways could consultants help build broken organizations from bottom-up?
e. List and explain at least five (5) best ways managers could develop plans of opportunities for learning and growth in organizations.
f. Are performance appraisals the most ideal way for motivating employees to give off their best? What other ways could be more effective and efficient in getting best outcomes?
g. Do management need inputs from employees to tailor rewards to individual needs? Why or why not?

IDEATION III

(With Grant, Jeff, Steve, John, & Vincent)

Diversity: Motivating Women to Achieve Success in Consulting

GRANT, A COST management consultant with CM/PG Cost Management Consulting Group believes that a consultant has to love her work and the travels. Jeff, an engineer and a marketing consultant believes that in most organizations, each department speaks different language with little collaboration among themselves. Steve, an international organizational development consultant specializes in people's development, and has passion for change. John, a prison director with twenty (20) years of experience working with the corrections facilities consults for both private and public sectors. John believes that government in many ways is dysfunctional on how money is spent, especially in the client-based consorting of prison facilities.

Vincent is the president of Global Lead, a large global specialty consulting firm. Vincent is an international diversity consultant, and believes the absolute resources for every organization is the people. The plenary dialogue began with the meaning of diversity. There was a consensus by the panelists that *"diversity is all the nouns that make us similar or different"*. Interestingly, the word "inclusion" came up in the discussion, and Vincent definition was: *"it is a process which enables us to get diversity out of the workplace"*. Indisputably, inclusive environment brings better results, but the process is not easy. An inclusive environment is not tension free, and tension they say, is life due to the passions and emotions attached to it.

It was clear among the panelists that there is no instant solution to the complex challenge of inclusion. Consulting panaceas like sensitivity training, diversity training, quotas, affirmative actions, and job enrichment works to some extent. A little bit of history from Robbins (2002) will clarify the issue:

> *The 1970s brought in centralized strategic planning, matrix organizational designs, management by committee, flextime, and zero-based budgeting. The 1980s gave us quality circles, and self-managed teams. The 1990s offered up personnel strategic alliances, exploiting core competencies, pay for competence, reengineering, mass customization, emotional intelligence, learning organizations, and empowerment (Robbins, 2003, pp. 195-197).*

The 2000s and beyond has a lot of uncertainties, impulsiveness, "connecting the dots" and the unquestionable truth that our world is now interconnected. It will demand a lot of anticipations and perfect calculations of the hidden cultures of organizations to succeed as a consultant. Just as a carpenter cannot solve every problem with a hammer, or my father-in-law (who happens to be a professional painter) cannot solve every painting job with a single brush, management cannot solve every inclusion and diversity problem with shortcuts and the old notes from college. Consultants need to treat new ideas and concepts of diversity as tools they can use to be able to read in-between the lines; be more discerning, and to maintain a consistent and fair organizational practice.

Another discussed issue was the complexity of consultants making their findings known in a way acceptable by both management and employees. Here, the panelists' concluded with a convincing tone that "the process is a science and art." The consultant needs to help management share data of what she found through her consulting facilitation. The consultant should also present data obtained through the consulting process to leaders/managers without fear or favor to set off the tone for a desired change. John quickly made a statement that "*a good manager should always get outside the chain to dig up the right feedback because most people are not courageous to share reality with management for fear of losing their jobs.*" I could not agree more!

A student asked an interesting question of how more women can be motivated to be successful in consulting. The responses were interesting. First, Jeff said "*talent always finds its own level*". Personally, I think the best way for talent to find its level is for one to believe in one's capabilities; work to improve upon one's skills and confidence, build networks, and connect with what one loves to do. Then, one can identify oneself to that particular organization of interest. This is a personal observation: Success in a profession is facilitated or hindered by the existence or absence of support resources. Yes! Competency could overawe artificial barriers when one performs beyond expectations, but no matter how motivated a person is, her performance and success is going to suffer if there isn't a supportive environment.

Motivation theorists and concept proponents such as Abraham Maslow – Hierarchy of needs; B.F. Skinner – Operant Conditioning, Frederick Herzberg – Motivation and Hygiene Theory, Douglas McGregor – Theory X and Theory Y, David McClelland – Acquired

Needs Theory, Victor Vroom – Expectancy Theory, and J. Stacy Adams – Equity Theory, all seems to agree that given our needs, choices, experiences on the job, positive management beliefs in employees, individuality of achievement, opportunity to weigh options, and fair treatment, most, if not all, employees will seize the opportunity to greatly enhance their performance (Williams, 2018). The point is, if managers do not give employees the chance and freedom to perform according to their abilities and skill set, consultants would be wasting their time in fixing the intangibles.

This is evident in most sports team benched players. Since these players don't get the opportunity and support of their coaches to play, they get "rusted" even though they possess the skill and talent to play. Even average players who consistently play games because the coaches have confidence in them and support them can perform to the best of their abilities and become stars. This scenario also helps to explain, for instance, why some employees with modest knowledge and skills consistently outperform and outshine others who are more endowed with knowledge, skills, and talents. The supportive environment could be lacking for the non-performing employees than the performing ones.

There is an impressive body of evidence that tells us that potential clients do not only look at absolute rewards, but relative rewards. They compare what inputs the consultant brings to the organization in terms of experience, effort, education, competence, and a relation building with the consultant's charging fee, recognition, and so forth. Then, the organization looks around for other references and referrals of consultants in similar fields to compare. Finally, the organizations evaluate the input/expected outcome ratio with other consultants and assess how equitably the consultant in question is being rewarded. I believe it is not what one gets out of consulting that should motivate one to be successful, but what one gives.

Exercises

a. State and explain five (5) tangible and intangible receivables that could motivate a consultant to be more successful.
b. State and explain five (5) tangible and intangible benefits a consultant can give to organizations to make them successful.
c. How important is supportive environment to a business success? Explain with examples.

IDEATION IV

(With Joan, Bob, Wendy, & Mark)

Customer Service: How Consultants Spend Time on a given Assignment.

THIS SESSION STARTED with a video clip. The clip taught me the simple truth of service, and remembered me the words of Henry Ford: "Coming together is a beginning, staying together is a process, working together is a success." Joan, a customer service specialist and trainer of employees to sustain positive behaviors begun by saying that **the consulting market leads one to where one is good at.** Joan belongs to an association called National Speakers Association to network as an external consultant. She stated that "if one has evidence of one's expertise through books, journals, blog, and a website, it will open doors for one as a consultant." Her reasons are that a consultant has to know her subject and the industries that hire those subjects (talent) to succeed.

Bob, also a customer service specialist believes one has to pay more attention to the customer. Bob argued that not all managers have the wisdom to let a consultant succeed in solving a challenge in an organization. He elaborated that some managers view the whole consulting process as avenue to seemingly prove their commitment to the employees but the managers are not committed to implementing the findings, more especially if the managers were the cause of the problem. For me, this piece of information should be a watchful grey area for all consultants. Wendy, a Human Resources career professional, trains and consults on organizational development. As an internal consultant, she concentrates on coaching, succession planning, and employees' development. She posited that *coaching entails listening modes to help employees identify what their needs are.* Wendy believes that it is better for a consultant to work for organizations whose mission resonates with hers.

Mark, a public and private operations consultant for 33 years had this to say: "If you get yourself in a situation that is not good for you, you need to change". What this statement means to me is that consultants, leaders, managers, and employees should find something they are happy doing and build their lives around it. From questions posed to the guests, these were the emerging themes:

a. Customer service for private sectors and public sectors are different.
b. Anywhere a consultant goes, he or she should learn history of the business first.
c. Everyday, consultants should prove their value to justify being there.
d. Consultants have to be adaptable to change to succeed in work of consulting, and read a lot on the subject of their consulting specialties.
e. While internal consultants see conflicts as perpetual occurrence and resolve to put different organizational puzzles together, external consultants have to build rapport and relations with the people.

f. Consultants should not act as "known all", but should ask the right questions and be genuine about themselves and their ignorance on an issue at stake.

There was also an interesting topic of how consultants spend time on a given project or assignment. Joan's response was more appealing to me:

"For the first few days, explore and discover the company; do mini-customer survey, assess both internal and external customer survey (internal and external existing data), process the pieces of information gathered and put them together for the training. Deliver by asking appropriate questions, evaluate, and train a trainer at the end of a consulting period so that she can continue from where you left off and follow-up".

Personally, I believe consultants need to master both the human and professional side of their work. Dr. Manning made a great statement: **"Every great consultant is always on time before even the people arrive."** It will always resonate in my mind that a good example of customer service is when the consultant waits for the people, not the other way around. The message here is that consultants need to be time conscious, smart, personable, decisive, verbally adept, and consistent in their consulting business. If one can successfully project these traits, one will increase the likelihood that her customers and colleagues will view her as an effective consultant.

Exercises

a. In your estimation, what are five important traits of a good customer service?
b. List and explain six attributes of a good consultant. Give practical examples to support your claims.

c. Should it be a rule or norm for every great consultant to always be on time before even the people arrive? Explain.
d. If you were a consultant, how would you spend time on a given project or assignment? This analysis should clearly state five (5) steps you would go through on a given consulting project or assignment.

IDEATION V

(With Bob, Jenny, and Marins)

Coaching:
Biggest Risk of Managers Today

BOB HAS ENORMOUS experience in corporate training for Fortune 500 companies; Jenny, a director of Tri-Health and a registered nurse for twenty (20) years trains in leadership development and has even built a leadership academy. **Marins has done all sorts of menial jobs before building his own company and a private consulting firm.** Most of the discussions of this session centered on coaching of managers to improve their performance. Marins believe **the biggest risk for managers today is <u>irrelevancy</u>**. He stated, "Barriers that protect incumbents in the past have broken down, and competitive positions can be quickly overturned". Bob also argued that if a manager misses a trend, there may be no catching up.

The question on the floor was: How does the manager stay out of the band of mediocrity and position herself to become an architect of managing revolution? The answer from Jenny was for the manager to reinvent who she is in a meaningful way.

A student called the panelists attention to the fact that most mangers still rely on their secretaries or personal assistants for typing of reports which can move back and forth in editing and counter editing. In addition, some managers cannot change simple printing sheets in modern printers, or attach a scanned document on a file, and remains quite old-fashioned. Technology and innovation are now deeply embedded in everything managers do in organizations, and being willing and able to handle these challenges are required for wealth creation and keeping managers at their jobs. The panelists nodded their heads in agreement. Jenny clarified her agreement (head-nodding) by stating that as organizations move beyond incremental change, strategic technological innovation becomes a key factor to renew its lease on success, and this largely depends on the managers who lead these organizations.

Suarez, Orozco, and Sattin (2008) suggested some of today's management competencies:

   a. Critical thinking skills in interdisciplinary judgment.
   b. Communication skills in intercultural understanding.
   c. Language skills in multilingual management
   d. Collaborative skills in facilitating, and
   e. Technology skills in information literacy across the organization.

Based on Suarez et al., (2008) suggestion above, I believe managers can be coached to be at their best, but only they themselves can reshape how they lead and change situations. The key here is a crafty blending of knowledge, creativity, productive learning of the employees, technology, and intellectual character in the company's mission. Managers should strive to actively involve all employees in the process to gain and give growth opportunities; develop a shared vision with a common ongoing goal for progress, assess each employee's needs, and create a positive future for themselves. Ultimately, **the employees should have a sense of**

dual belonging: Privilege of belonging, and responsibility of belonging.

Ford and Haar (2008) provided these guiding questions for managers to explore:

  a. How do we create effective teams for our employees?
  b. How do we influence change in a practical way?
  c. What conditions are needed for effective group thinking?
  d. How do we build interdependent relationships?
  e. How can we increase interpersonal and team skills?
  f. How do we ensure individual and team accountability?
  g. How do we develop commitment to a common purpose?

I believe the heart of all these important questions is to build strength in the organization for growth, sustainability, and success. However, I do not believe managers should be coached to build strength with only like-minded people. There is a saying that if everybody in the organization is thinking the same, then, no one is thinking. There is beauty in diversity of ideas. It builds passion for growth.

Finally, as consultants coach managers to use multiple measures to understand the multifaceted world of management from the perspective of all employees involved, consultants should have at the back of their minds that most modern managers are "immigrants" as compared to the "Net generation" (those born from 1980 are called Net Generation). The Net Generation can really multitask and are more technology savvy. To keep it simple, management coaching should help the manager create a culture of accountability by looking at the process rather than the results. Bernhardt (2009) in his book, "*Data, data everywhere*" points to vital needs of words such as 'process', 'demographics', 'perceptions', and "employees' outcome" as the yardstick in attaining a given outcome. **The big idea is to know how to peel the onion.**

Exercises

a. "The biggest risk for managers today is irrelevancy." Agree/Disagree. Explain in two paragraphs.
b. How do managers stay out of the band of mediocrity and position themselves to become architects of managing revolution?
c. How do managers create effective teams for employees?
d. Why should managers influence change in a practical way? Give practical example to support your positionality.
e. What conditions are needed for effective group thinking?
f. How do we build interdependent relationships at the workplace?
g. How can managers increase interpersonal and team skills in organizations?
h. How do managers ensure individual and team accountability?
i. Analyze three ways management can develop commitment to a common purpose?

IDEATION VI

(With Hank, Gordon, and Steve)

How to Unravel Problems during Consulting

HANK (DR.) BEGUN this discussion by stating that he is broadly involved in pre-employment type situations developing professional growth plans for individuals through attitude moral surveys and one-on-one management coaching in Human Resources for variety of organizations. Gordon also introduced himself as an independent consultant for fifteen (15) years in helping people in the fundamental story of change. Steve, on the other hand, after twenty-seven (27) years in the U.S. Army, is now a leadership consultant in the transportation business and works as a Human Resources Generalist at Metro Bus in downtown Cincinnati, Ohio.

Discussions from this plenary session had the following emerging themes:

   a. Consultants should be non-theoretical in their consulting approach. They should be more practical in trying to understand the people they work for.

b. How well a consultant knows herself helps in building an effective change model.
c. Consultants should get a good alignment of what success looks like because individuals see success in different ways.
d. A good consultant gives more than what is expected, and tries to execute her work in such a manner that all stakeholders are satisfied.
e. A good consultant also builds on the foundations of her Emotional Intelligence (EI) through self-awareness.
f. Organizational development should begin from individuals to the executive level.
g. Good consultants concentrate on visual presentation; know what they are talking about, be what they say they are, and do what they talk about.

One important and interesting issue that hit me during the discussion was how to unravel problems during the consulting business so that appropriate tools would be devised to solve those problems. The answer from Gordon was that **consultants have to keep constant eye on what is going on at the *systemic level*, *group level*, and the *individual level* in every consulting assignment**. According to the panelists, consultants need to know all these three levels to be able to handle any organizational challenge. Here, Gordon convinced me with the assertion that, **"when the problem is a systemic one, then, it is a leadership, service, and professional connection issue."** The bottom line is that when such situation happens, individual level problems cannot be solved unless all the others (systemic and group levels) have been dealt with.

I believe the challenge is how the consultant converts her intentions on the issues presented into an actionable one with physical results. From my personal consulting experience, sensitivity is key: Know your clients, what their needs are, and do it for them. **Consultants have to stretch their patience a little bit to know where the edge is and must listen.** As an example, problem solving in organizations have always been a complex set of ongoing interactions between and among consultants, managers, and employees within the context of each organization's culture and climate. Consultants only need to take a little bit of time to study the history and narrations of any organization they have agreed to work with; study the pattern, follow the flow, and help the people to change from within. Margaret Whitley got this one right: "There is no power for change greater than a community discovering what it cares about.

Exercises

a. "There is no power for change greater than a community discovering what it cares about." Agree/Disagree. Explain.
b. How can consultant be non-theoretical in their consulting approach, but practical?
c. As a consultant, demonstrate how you will try to understand the people you work for.
d. "How well a consultant knows herself helps in building an effective change model." Agree/Disagree. Explain.
e. Analyze how consultants can get a good alignment of what success looks like in business, when individual businesses see success in different ways.
f. As a good consultant, how can you give more than what is expected, and try to execute your work in such a manner that all stakeholders are satisfied.
g. Do you think good consultants should build on their foundations of Emotional Intelligence (EI) through self-awareness? Why or why not?
h. Is it appropriate for business Organizational Development to begin from individuals to the executive level? Explain your positionality.
i. "Good consultants concentrate on visual presentation; know what they are talking about, be what they say they are, and do what they talk about." Agree/Disagree. Explain.

IDEATION VII

(With Dale, Tom, Beverley, Greg, Steve, and Mike)

How Do Students Enter into the Consulting Field?

DALE, AN IT programmer and CEO of an organization called *Instructional Development*, is an internal consultant. Tom, an external consultant, consults for all kinds of businesses (property management, plastics, manufacturing, processing, etc.) and specializes in operations. Beverly is the Director of a Tennessee based Human Rights Commission, and has consulted for most fortune 500 companies. Greg Love has worked many years for the YMCA, and has been in many profit and non-profit organizations as external consultant. Mike (Dr.) is an Organizational Development consultant.

I realized that each of the panelists have different passions of the job they do as consultants. For instance, Beverly is passionate about people and community building. Greg has a passion for cultural change in organizations. Dale has passion for leadership development functions in the hospitality industry, while Tom's passion is to provide merchandize for the food and processing industries. Mike on the other hand, after trying many consulting fields, has found a passion for executive coaching. He works with teams of senior executives to become more effective by working with them individually and in groups.

For me, the major question and most interesting one on the floor was "How do students enter into the consulting field?"

These were the exciting responses from the panelists:

a. Start from the entry level
b. Begin to get more insights into sales, pre-sales, and support techniques by integrating with other functions of sales.
c. Keep your eyes open and build on your experience.
d. One can gain experience into consulting not only from working, but volunteering.
e. Look for the things you have passion for, and build your experience on that.
f. Follow your passion and talent.
g. Keep your finger on the pulse of your own life, follow it, and you'll find your passion in consulting.
h. It depends on what you have to offer and who you are going to offer that to.
i. One can partner with others and share knowledge and skills.
j. We can offer people our own life story in "knowing what we know."
k. One can start working for a large consulting firm and learn from the job.
l. Begin to look for internal consultant's position at your current work place.

Among all the responses, the one I found in consonance with my experience as a consultant is the response by Greg. Greg said, "**Before you will know how to enter into consulting, ask yourself what consulting mean to you?**"

Basically, most students who want to go into consulting need self-awareness. They need to know what is in them that others love; figure out the language of what people want, and develop a strategy to work on it. Even though knowledge and professional experience is paramount in consulting, I have come to believe that good consultants tend to have experience doing a job and doing it well for some time before going out on their own to consult. Depending on the field of consulting, one will need some sort of experience, or a story (all our knowledge and experiences are stories anyway) to prove our competency. During consulting, clients will most of the time ask questions to test a consultant's authority on the issue under discussion or her competency for the job she is performing, and the consultant need to make a case to convince her clients why she is qualified to do that job at that particular moment. The consultant also needs to be good at marketing herself; network effectively, be self-reliant and good at thinking on her feet in understanding her clients' problems and needs, and help the clients come out with solutions. This sort of creative problem-solving can be the most rewarding part of consulting.

Additionally, after the consultant has decided on her consulting path, she needs a business plan. A plan put into writing of where she wants to go, and how she wants to get there.

The plan should spell out the services she wants to offer, who she thinks will buy her services, how big or small her market is, what resources we will be needed and what personal qualifications she needs to have to meet the challenges? One of the panelists, Dale, made a comment that I agree perfectly: "When a consultant forget about money, she makes money". If one intends to go into consulting with money as a sole or major objective, one is bound not to realize her dreams. Commitment to relationship building, character, trust building, and paying attention to intangibles like energy, morale, timing, and momentum will bring the money.

Exercises

a. As a consultant, give a comprehensive and detailed advice to students who want to enter into the consulting field.
b. "When a consultant forgets about money, she makes money". Do you agree or disagree with this statement? Explain.
c. Analyze how a consultant can also be a good marketer of the profession.
d. List and explain five (5) intangibles that a consultant should pay attention to.
e. When a business says a consultant is competent, what competencies comes to your mind? List and explain five of them.
f. Why is self-awareness such an important word to anyone wanting to be a consultant?

IDEATION VIII

(With Sue, George, Gail, and Phil)

The Future of Consulting is the Knowledge of Change.

THIS GROUP, LIKE other group of panelists, were also diversified in gender and experience. Sue started as a high school history teacher for ten years before entering into consulting. Gail, George and Phil have all done at least three different jobs before finally settling on consulting. Their passion also varies from organizational development to succession planning. What excited me about this discussion was a point made by Sue that "**The future of consulting is knowledge of change.**"

I noticed while consulting in a project that even small clients (of say ten people) have developed roles, rights, and rituals to differentiate its members. As an example, e-mail among the team has to follow an up and down hierarchical line with different tones and styles necessitated by managers and subordinates. In this case, traditional authority levels have to be observed. For example, the manager tended to send short and curt messages to subordinates, in part to minimize contact with them, but also to convey comfort of her authority. In contrast, if a subordinate sends a similar short e-mail as a response to the manager, it tends to be misinterpreted as being rude.

Due to some of these subtle issues that may take time and effort before the consultant can even get to know before understanding, the consultant need to be acquainted with what groups are; differentiate between groups (as in formal and informal groups), recognize group dynamics and how to analyze group interactions, identify how role requirements change in different situations, how norms exert influence on individuals behavior in group settings, and contrast the effectiveness of interacting, brainstorming, nominal, and electronic meeting groups in order to grasp the foundations of dealing with the change process. My point here is that consultants should not look at management or employees in isolation. Rather, they should assess the degree of support provided to employees by management and external conditions before helping them in the change process. This will ensure sustainability.

I presume many organizations believe in ethic of individuals; value achievement, and recognize it as such. Likewise, **many individuals enjoy being part of a group in which they can maintain a strong individual identity**. Research has shown that most employees do not enjoy substituting their identity to that of the group and this is where many managers don't get it. Leadership literatures show that most employees appreciate a clear link between their individual effort and a visible outcome. Every organization (unless may be, the leader belongs to another planet), wants to breed achievers, and the secret is that most achievers seek personal responsibility even in a group setting. "They will be frustrated in job situations in which their contribution is commingled and homogenized with the contribution of others." (Robinson, 2008, p. 248).

It seems plausible that almost every rational being actively seeking a job wants to be hired, evaluated, and rewarded on their individual achievements. Some tend to believe in authority and status hierarchy; accept a system in which there are bosses and subordinates, and are not likely to accept groups decision on issues as their job assignments and wage increases. It will even be harder yet to imagine that they will be comfortable in a system in which the sole basis for their promotion or termination would be the performance of their group, yet, we continue to preach that all jobs should be designed around groups. I remember the title of H.J. Leavitt book written in 1975 in the wake of our panelists' discussion on change which is more relevant today: *"Suppose we took groups seriously"*. Consultants need to understand that helping to change institutions, and corporate culture is an ongoing process, which takes time and requires a new approach that has the power to reverse the trend of external direction in every individual and help leaders bring up empathetic, self-confident, moral, and group-thinkers who have the ability to hold each others hand to succeed. Consultants can help in this direction by transforming organizations from continuous assumptions, values, and patterns of behavior of people towards creating a desired group-work of individual effort environment. That way, low performers who hide behind the group can be spotted and helped.

Exercises

a. Do passion play a part in being a good consultant? Explain.
b. Leadership is helping to change organizations and corporate culture in an ongoing process. Agree/Disagree. Explain.
c. Leadership literatures show that most employees like a clear link between their individual effort and a visible outcome. Do you agree or disagree with this statement? Explain.
d. As a consultant how would you create a desired group-work of individual effort environment?

IDEATION IX

(With Matt, David, and Margaret)

Marketing in its Real Sense

MATT (DR.) IS a business Dean of a major public university in Ohio, USA. Margaret is involved in civic engagements, and started her own consulting business in 2003. David on the other hand, studied political science, and consults in public administration because he has held many local government positions. David had been the administrator of a big County in Ohio for several years before entering into consulting.

The themes that emerged from discussions with this group of panelists were:

    a. **Consultants need Tolerance, Talent and Technology (*3 Ts*).**
    b. Managers should plan to give employees permission to say no.
    c. Identify your competition because your competition may become your partner.
    d. Write professional articles, speak at conferences, and write books on your field of consulting to make yourself valuable.

e. There is highs and lows in consulting. You can be fired.
f. Everyone in the organization adds value, and that is why they were hired. They help immensely in paying managers and leaders salaries. If they are not there, management will simply not function.
g. Building long-term partnership at the workplace without balance, fit, wants, and uniqueness will make the partnership short-lived.

Matt concentrated on marketing in its real sense. He defined marketing as "The process of planning, executing conception, pricing, promotion and distribution of goods, services, and ideas to create exchanges that satisfy individuals and organizational goals". According to Matt, pricing a consulting service is a marketing decision. He elaborated on the "4 P's" of marketing consulting services – Product, Pricing, Promotion, and Place (location). This is how Matt framed his marketing strategy.

External Factors	Planning	Internal Factors
• Competition • Legal/political • Demographics • Technology • Culture • Physical environment • Economy	• Understand consumers and markets • SWOT analysis • Marketing research • Market selection decisions • Service provided • Pricing • Promotion • Place • Implementation Control: • Timing • Relationship • Achieving goals • Advertising	• Your Vision • Your Mission • Your Objectives • Marketing goals

The "4P" planning framework is a marketing tool that helps to develop a "market all the time" attitude. This framework gives a know-how guide to develop and implement a dynamic marketing plan that will make consulting business more visible to clients and more competitive in the marketplace. As an inexpensive and effective marketing tool, it will help direct a consultant's focus on marketing aspects of consulting in the following areas:

    a. Developing a successful marketing plan.
    b. Understanding the marketing ins and outs of an individual consulting firm.
    c. Find new clients.
    d. Develop more creative marketing ideas.
    e. Retain existing clients, and

f. Project quality in consulting training materials through marketing research to inform prospects about our consulting.

I realized through this marketing framework that knowing how to frame issues will let many consultants be more effective in marketing a consultancy services; increase success in implementing goals, and get clients agreement on many issues of common interest and importance because once the right frames are in place, the right behavior will follow.

In addition, consultants need to frame problems in common ways to prevent cultural misunderstanding.

Exercises

a. Do you think Consultants need Tolerance, Talent and Technology (*3 Ts*)? Discuss.
b. Why is it important for managers to plan to give employees permission to say no?
c. As a consultant, why is there a need to identify your competition because your competition may become your partner?
d. Is there a need for consultants to write professional articles, speak at conferences, and write books on their field of consulting to make them valuable? Discuss.
e. "Building long-term partnership at the workplace without balance, fit, wants, and uniqueness will make the partnership short-lived." Agree/Disagree. Discuss.

IDEATION X

(With Dr. Jeff alone)

Consultants are like Actors on a Stage

JEFF HAS BEEN with Great American Insurance for over thirty years as a consultant, and has been teaching at a public university for sixteen (16) years. He is an internal consultant; teaches leadership in both graduate and undergraduate classes, builds customized and standardized core programs, has consulted extensively in the U.S and China, and passionate about changing behaviors and getting results.

These were the themes of the discussion with Jeff:

a. External consultants do not have ownership of what they leave behind after consulting.
b. A consultant should not always be a fun of theory. She should believe in practical ways of managing a team in a time-tested proven way.
c. Emotional Intelligence competencies are essential in today's consulting.

d. The focus of consulting should be on clients and customer service.
e. Consulting in a different country works better when the consultant put the people in groups.
f. Never train or coach a leadership team when you don't have an action plan.
g. Let your clients pick one new idea everyday in your organizational consulting.
h. A consultant should always seek reactions and impressions from her clients.
i. Part of both internal and external consultant's job is sales, and the other part is delivering on results.
j. Leaders and consultants should have the highest possible integrity, and earn people's trust before they can gain respect.

The most interesting thing for me on this discussion was when Jeff said, "**Consultants are like actors.**" According to him, **organizations pay consultants money to stand in front of them to perform.** Hear him: "**You want your clients (audience) to learn, be entertained, and be informed to take something home – you better give them something worth their money.**"

I believe Jeff's contention is true, but to be a good "actor" as a consultant, entails a lot of behind the stage preparation, especially, external consultants. How do we, as external consultants, go about marketing our services to become "star-actors" or celebs? How do we develop a marketing plan? What about networking, corporate image, and consistent message for our clients? **Remember to never train a team of managers or people without an action plan.**

I believe a preparatory solution is for some consultants to get their consulting business on the web to establish their presence and concentrate on the most important marketing of networking.

A serious consultant should find a way to be known to potential clients and seek referrals or vendors, which to me is a delicate but most crucial business of consulting. Those who do it best know its value. Doing better research on the organization we are about to consult for; working on a passionate topic that will resonate with most employees, improving targeting, and updating training tools and manuals which deepens content and produces efficient consulting results will also market a particular consultant.

I have consistently made my intentions clear from the introduction of these reflections that situations differ on each "stage" that a consultant performs. The consultant's job in each situation is to compensate for things lacking in an organization or the work setting by concentrating on leader-employee relations, group norms, the organization's culture, and leadership expectations. Thus, the consultant's effectiveness to her clients will depend on how well she can identify these factors that are lacking, and her ability to fill those gaps on the 'stage' as she performs to her audience.

Exercises

a. Are consultants actually like actors on the stage? Why or why not?
b. "External consultants do not have ownership of what they leave behind after consulting." Discuss.
c. The focus of consulting should be on clients and customer service. Why is this not always the case?
d. Consulting in a different country works better when the consultant put the people in groups. How would you do this effectively as a consultant?
e. Never train or coach a leadership team when you don't have an action plan. Create an action plan for a leadership team of your choice.
f. As a consultant, demonstrate how you will seek reactions and impressions from your business clients.
g. Part of both internal and external consultant's job is sales, and the other part is delivering on results. Which part is easier, sales or delivering on results? Explain.

IDEATION XI

The 39th Consultant: Insights from the Class

THE FIELD OF consulting entails preparation, attitude, skills, and personal principles. It is up to the consultant to learn the products, processes, problems, principles and practices of each organization she wants to consult for. There will always be the consultant lens, stories, and lessons learned in each consulting assignment. The consultant should decide on what she could o best and want to do most. It can be training and development, personnel selection, assessment, labor relations, executive coaching or anything one has great interest in. The consultant should specialize in about three services and eight areas of expertise that would be enjoyable and doable in consulting.

Services could be presentations, facilitations (planning, teambuilding, and problem-solving), or professional/management development (seminars and coaching). The eight areas of expertise could be morale, productivity, ethics, motivation, stress, communication, group dynamics, and leadership. The consultant should use time management principles based on values, yearly goals, and daily "to do" check list and execute a daily work regimen – every working day, do something for an old client, another for a new client, and yet another for a prospective client. It could be a call, sending a book, solving problem, email, or thank you card.

Five Finger Consulting.

According to Manning (2009) there is an absolute need to live and work by five core principles of consulting success:

a. Focus on mission and values vs. style and techniques (quality of work/quality of work life), and put clients interests first.
b. Tell the truth as you see it.
c. Keep organizational knowledge current.
d. Plan and prepare, but remain flexible.
e. Deliver results.

Another insight from this course was that teaching and practical professional experience helps consulting. A consultant who teaches and practices the profession grows through professional challenges; learns the functions and settings of organizations, customizes herself with behavioral and business practice learning, and learning the business of business. Writing on the field of consulting also helps in living and working in a challenging world of consulting. In all situations, the consultant should use her brain and the terrain in creating a niche. Sometimes, consulting partnership is necessary where one plus one could be more than two.

Mistakes of omission and commission should be expected. Documents would be lost, some nights would provide only bad sandwiches to eat, but consultants can learn and teach from those dramatic experiences for the right reasons (morale and productivity), in the right way (other's interest first), and enough money will follow. So how much should you charge? No more than you would be happy to pay. Sex can sell for sexual consultants, but never do it if your conscience does not serve you right. Every consultant should document a list of most challenging assignment, most physical group, most dangerous clients, most glamorous assignments, most unusual story, most political group, and most appreciative group she has consulted for.

The consultant should familiarize herself with cross-cultural communication and business success. **She should also train trainers who would continue with the consulting process in the consultant's absence to help the people in the organization through change.**

There are red flags: The most stressful groups to consult for may be physicians who are handling frenzy, frustrations and fatigue; attorneys, political organizations, dissatisfied teachers, and financial officers. There is always the likelihood of what the consultant didn't know that she didn't know that she wishes she knew. Hidden agenda of managers and leaders of organizations should be watchful grey areas.

Finally, how do you change others? You don't they do – and then if you preach the way they want to be or teach knowledge and skill they chose to use, they would gradually change and follow your path. People do what they want when the consultant is not there. Be a cautious learner of leadership, teambuilding, quality, power of vision, stress and change, and ethics. Remember, evaluation criteria for organizational interventions could be pace, relevance, value or participation. Join professional organizations and use outdoor activities for relationship building and networking.

Exercises

a. How do consultants change managers and employees in organizations they consult for? Do they really change them or bring the best in them? Explain.
b. How much should a consultant charge on a given assignment and why? What factors should go into the fee?
c. What are four factors that make consultants focus on mission and values as well as style and techniques to enhance quality of work of clients?
d. When we say consultants should tell the truth as they see it, what do you think are some of the truths untold?
e. Analyze four ways consultants can keep organizational knowledge current? Explain four factors.
f. As a consultant how do you Plan and prepare, but remain flexible in delivering results?

FINAL IDEATIONS

Sitting Home Alone: Leadership is Key.

CHANGE IS TAKING place with such a speed that traditional consulting, training, and coaching continues to struggle to keep up with the exploding proliferation of innovation and technology, while social revolution of distrust between management and employees sweeps in behind it. Distrust in leadership is widespread. The *New York Times* in early 2009 reported that 72 percent of employees feel that wrongdoing is widespread in industries. A recent *Business Week* poll showed that only 33 percent of Americans feel large companies have ethical business practices; just 26 percent believe management is straightforward and honest in their dealing with others, and 79 percent believe corporate America put their own personal interests ahead of workers' and shareholders'. Further, 88 percent of consumers distrust big companies, and 76 percent of employees have observed illegal or unethical behavior from their employer in the past twelve months (Williams, 2019).

Organizations and communities, they say, are products of the ways the people in them think and interact. As consultants play their part in charting a framework of leadership that yields not only a richer and healthier world, but absolute trust in leadership, the path of trust should be a straight one, not the usual twisted one we all know. Leadership roles in organizational projects, programs, and activities have become complex, daunting, and overwhelming. Nevertheless, transparency in leadership is vital in surviving today's competitive and volatile economy. In a world where confidence in business leadership is at a low point (Marre, 2009), consultants must play pivotal roles by bringing a unique passion in their training, coaching, and consulting that inspires leaders to change through the modeling of a trustworthy working environment by first, challenging leaders to transform their thinking, goals formulation, and strategies.

Fred Harburg, former President of Motorola University has recently challenged organizational leaders at YouTube to "think new thoughts and act new ways." According to Marre (2009), **"current developments illustrates our society's toxic distrust of leaders, and that, sometimes things are so broken to an extent that compromise creates only an illusion of progress"**. (p. 22)

When consultants move to an organization to consult, what do they find? An organization which is gender inclusive and ethnically sensitive? Do these organizations reflect demographic reality without a sense of hostility and competitiveness of cultural clamoring?

The globalization of technology, communication, and constant travels of consultants all over the world has made their reality a culturally diverse environment that begs the question "who trust who?" How do we wake up one cock-crow and suddenly there are minorities in our neighborhood? And as if that is not enough, we find, on that same day, that there are more women, immigrants, and people with accents at the workplace, and we know little to nothing about how to interact with them or be culturally sensitive to them. These new demographic realities should change the way consultants think, act, and bring their expertise to bear on a given organization to enhance trust.

Max De Pree, in *Leadership is an Art*, states, "The first responsibility of a leader is to define reality." (p. 2). This assertion directly relates to consultants in defining reality at the workplace because most external consultants know relatively little about the organizations they seek to bring change. Before consultants can meet the expectations of their clients and enhance trust after a consulting assignment at a particular organization is over, consultants need a master plan. The rapid compression of time in consulting; ability to process events, and the urgency of answers to complex organizational challenges are demanded by clients at the touch of a key stroke. The information age is juxtaposed against the "relationship desire." A lot of what consultants' mirror depends on the management of that organization. That means there are certain areas of focus that the consultant needs to comprehend if she wants to meet the challenges of the rapidly changing mosaic of a society and workplace of ours. One of the core areas is "distrust of leadership."

Distrust in Retrospective

According to Bailey (2002), distrust or lack of trust for leadership, is one of the reasons why people resist change. In a related study, Kervonen & Parkkinen (2001) found that lack of trust has been repeatedly identified as one of the most formidable barriers to the process of change. Trust, is defined in the *William Webster's Collegiate Dictionary, Eleventh Edition (2007)* as "assured resilience on character, to place confidence in, to commit or place in one's care or keeping, veracity, reliability, or the truth of a statement." Ironically, researchers have found it difficult to define trust despite Webster's definition.

Most researchers could only conceptualize trust to features of a particular context. This has led to many definitions of trust

(Husted, 1998; Sabol 2002; and Fukuyama (1995). The reasons for definitional differences are not far-fetched. First, trust is an abstract concept often used interchangeably with related concepts like credibility, reliability or confidence (Sabol, 2002; Lane & Klenke, 2004). Therefore, defining trust and delineating the distinction with its related concepts have proven challenging for researchers (Lane & Klenke, 2004). Second, trust is a multi-faceted concept that incorporates cognitive, affective, and behavioral dimensions (Lewis & Weigert, 1985). Thus, trust is widely studied in many academic and professional disciplines, but each discipline has its own understanding of the concept and different ways to operationalize it (Tannenbaum, 2003).

Nissenbaum (2001) summarized trust in this notion:

Trust is an extraordinarily rich concept covering a variety of relationships, conjoining a variety of objects. One can trust (or distrust) persons, institutions, governments, information, deities, physical things, systems, and more (p. 104).

Thus far, lack of consistent principle by which consultants can define trust and its manifestations as used in the leader-employee change relationship remains a challenge. I remember a couple of issues that caused lack of trust (distrust) between a project's team and the team leader when I worked in an international project as an external consultant. The team leader's inability to listen did not endear her to the team. She had no patience to listen to a staff member's side of the bargain, and leaves nobody in doubt that the final decision of every meeting or deliberation rests with her. Besides, she did not exhibit a sense of consistency in her dealings. For instance, she will ask her team to use existing operational tools for monitoring and evaluation of all consulting trainings, but will request another external consultant (without consulting her team) for a second opinion when the existing tools were working to perfection without any complaints whatsoever from any of her employees or clients. For me, there is nothing wrong with seeking second opinion of how a consulting training tool works with clients, but when a group perceives that the hiring of another consultant is a calculated attempt to check on their effectiveness and efficiency, with the team leader not being part of the "second opinion" process, it breeds suspicion and distrust.

Moreover, the team leader was not consistent in her articulation of the position of the project sponsor's sum of money voted for each phase of their consulting contract. Pay structure, traveling allowances, benefits, and vacations for example, was stated to be inclusive of one's salary yet, the team leader took traveling allowances for herself, personal secretary, and personal driver while all other team members did not receive such benefits. Assuming another external consultant comes to such an organization to consult on organizational development. Logically, even the team members will resist change because of distrust between the team and their leader. Machiavelli once said, "… but he, who, contrary to the will of the people, has become prince by the favor of the nobles, should at once and before everything else strive to win the goodwill of the people, which will be easy for him, by taking them under his protection". When we, as consultants are hired on a particular assignment (unknowingly contrary to the will of employees because they perceive leadership as the problem), we should strive to win the employees goodwill before they can trust our protection and open up to us of the real problems in their organization.

There is also the problem of employees' accessibility to organizational information. Such accessibility of information is instrumental to trust or distrust of leaders. For instance, if there is a policy of keeping one's salary secret, the question is, will it create suspicion of favoritism and the belief of unfairness among the team? The point I want to highlight for consultants here is that, a person's degree of trust, commonly called *individual trust propensity*, is a dynamic function of actions and consequences over time (Boyle & Bonicich, 1970; Diller, 2003).

I believe in the wisdom of Kouzes and Posner in their book, *Leadership Challenge*. They maintained that a leader must be able to model the way, inspire a shared vision, challenge the process, enable others to act, and encourage the heart to enhance trust (p. 12).

Consultants should know that in modeling the way, most managers in organizations are doing well, but they are not allowing their employees to find their voice by clarifying their individual personal values. Besides, most managers are not setting examples by aligning actions with shared values of their organization's code of conducts. Most of them live by the tenets of George Orwell's animal farm principles of "all animals are equal, but some are more equal than others". Moreover, some managers are not inspiring vision at their work places. Some cannot envision the future by imaging exciting and ennobling possibilities. They find it difficult to enlist team members and employees in a common vision and ignore shared aspirations.

Again, some managers find their subordinates who challenge the status quo as a challenge on their personal integrity. We are all aware that most employees search for opportunities by seeking innovative ways to change, grow, and improve. It is therefore, a surprise to some employees if they realize that management does not want to experiment many ideas or take further risks. The simple truth is that it is boring to work for a manager who does not grow. Most employees need their managers to grow in order to enable them to also grow and act, and to foster collaboration by promoting cooperative goals and building trust. Managers and leaders could do this by strengthening their teams through power sharing and discretion (Bailey, 2002). Unfortunately, that is not the case in many institutions and organizations most consultants consult for. Some managers use authoritative power and try to take advantage of every situation by appealing to employees' fears and emotions. Finally, one does not need to consult an oracle to know that some managers do not encourage the heart.

Little efforts demand encouragement so that the behavior can be repeated.

I consulted for an organization (name withheld for a purpose), where the group told me that any remarkable achievement from an employee will elicit this response from their manager: "That is why I am paying you good money." Apparently, an unfortunate attitude like this from a manager brings a situation where employees cannot celebrate the values and victories of individual accomplishments leading to lack of group spirit. What I did as a consultant was to recommend a one-week retreat on change management for that small organization of fifteen employees to find antidote to the endemic distrust.

I divided my training manuals into four parts:

- Contacting and contracting
- Participatory assessment
- Analysis of collected data and feedback to client system
- Legal and Institutional Framework Study

The initial stage of *contacting and contracting* was to meet all employees individually (each of them face-to-face) to access their knowledge, fears, aspirations, and expectations in the organization through a mini-survey.

The *participatory assessment* stage dealt with the retreat session in assessing the employees' skills, team spirit, personal dynamics, and shared vision in a role play and plenary sessions. Data was collected in the process to develop a comprehensive report as a blueprint of the way forward for the organization. I partnered with a renowned lawyer in the business of my clients to handle the legal aspect of the process.

My overall objective was to develop internal capacity and operational linkages with the team and other stakeholders, and to analyze all data to identify similarities, differences, expectations, and concerns that could either contribute to, or inhibit the trust-building process. We went through the process of dialogue in the participatory stage (listening, inquiring, reflecting, and advocating) to build relationships, roles, responsibilities, and procedures among the team to clarify and improve the situation of distrust. The process put the team in a better position to maximize their potentials within the organization, and a comprehensive plan to minimize or avoid risk of internal conflict.

In the *participatory retreat process*, I divided the team into three focus groups of four members in each group to complete standard assessment forms to capture each group's responses during plenary discussions. Before closing each day's activity, we conducted a final plenary by sharing all groups' assessment results. This particular closing activity was used to address issues/concerns, which needed immediate attention. At the overall focus group matrix report, some themes kept popping up in variations such as quantity and quality of communication. The focus group believed that quality of information leads to quality of relationship, which has a direct implication for team success, and sustainability of services. While not all of these examples applied to every location of a consultant's job, replicating the model can be helpful.

My effort paid off. I was able to discover the challenge: Between the team and their manager, better understanding of material costs related issues, benefits of members, transparency, clarity regarding pay structures, and petty cash to run daily recurring expenditure was of great concern. Between the manager and her immediate assistant, there was the issue of power sharing, commitment, time, and suspicion of "hidden agenda". Overall, the consulting process made us realize that there was the need for team members to support management and vice versa, and a feeling that individual's roles were understood and appreciated.

Bottom line, any suspicion of such issues as roles and responsibilities and appreciation erodes trust among the team. The retreat process transformed results positively. Both management and the employees realized that there was the need for collective commitment to change. However, it was clear that change was not an easy process, and becomes increasingly complex as more stakeholders were involved. Together with the management and the team, we **developed a roadmap based on the information, reflection, and results of the assessment.** That means developing a picture of the future, with new structures, policies, and methods based on the beliefs and values of all stakeholders, which will build the type of relationship and interactions so much desired in any team to enhance trust.

Actually, all that the organization had to do was to acknowledge past mistakes, and change policies which no longer work. The present was critically assessed, and all team members and management set a compelling future vision. Assumptions were questioned in an open manner; individual visions and values were aligned, and broad participation and team spirit enhanced. Slowly, but surely, not only the structures, procedures, and technology changed, but the team's level of knowledge of awareness, attitude, and in some cases values and beliefs as well. It was then that trust for the team and their managers come alive!

Recommendations

Cultural competency.

Every consultant must first help the management to examine their cultural programming. This introspective gaze must ask questions such as: Do I see myself as superior to others? Do I make assumptions that stereotype and pigeonhole people into self-fulfilling prophesies? Do I see employees with little education (manual workers) as less valuable? And how do I feel about diversity within the work environment? Questions like these get the ethnocentrism that sabotages managers' ability to allow the mission of an organization to lead through them. Challenging managers to connect the culture that has formed them with the culture that confronts them, without shutting down is the heart's task for managers' relation to culture, and a sure way of building trust. Besides knowing one's cultural programming, it is important for consultants to create the awareness for managers to understand the values, norms, and beliefs of other cultures in their organization.

Managers should pay regular visits to assembly lines or employees' cubicles and offices to familiarize themselves with situations on the ground by asking few questions; talking with individuals, who are open to discussing their worldview, group sharing, and other creative activities. This can foster dialogue in diversity and interpersonal discernment. Note that some individuals enjoy hiding in their own corner and do not appreciate bosses who pop into their offices unaware. Here, management should balance their visits with reasoning and act with prudence. The recommended interaction/visitation must be a part of every agenda. Employees must sense that they are valuable and needed at the workplace. Constant and purposeful communication must take place.

Milton Bennet, a cross-cultural specialist, stated:

> *Intercultural sensitivity is not natural ... nor has it characterized most of human history. Cross-cultural contact often has been accompanied by oppression. Today, the failure to exercise intercultural sensitivity is not simply bad business or bad morality – it is self-destructive. So, we face a choice: overcome the legacy of our history, or lose history itself for all time"* (p. 18).

Intentionality.

Ideas of self-reliance, individualism, and independence, so much admired in many of the traditions of significant segments of today's societies, will not dwell easily in projects where the consultant is trying to focus on collaboration, team work, and unity. It is the continued task of both management and the consultant to remind employees that the ground is level for everyone to succeed if one works smart and dedicates his/her efforts to the cause of the organization. Managers should also have the courage to overcome their own cultivated tendencies that tend to thwart the practice of egalitarianism in branch settings. The consultant should also help her clients to design their programs and visions to include the concept of all-inclusiveness.

As Oswald Sanders wrote, "We can lead others only as far long as the road we ourselves have traveled". **Merely pointing the way is not enough. If we are not walking, then no one can follow, and we are not leading anyone either.**

The idea of intentionality means that the concern for diversity issues is always on the agenda of the manager. What the manager sees as important becomes important for the organization and the employees. The reverse is true. That is why intentionality focuses on clear sense of direction which must come from the leader when negotiating the waters of multicultural complexity. Waves of complexity and conflict will swell from time to time in a pluralistic organization. The manager must use the power of intentionality in weaving a collective consciousness of her embracing diversity to minimize the potential struggle that comes with the challenges of a multicultural organizational environment.

Conflict mediation skills.

Every client's spirit is tested when facing conflict in an organization. It is especially important for managers of multicultural organizations to understand the basic conflict resolution skills across cultures. In his book, *Becoming a Healthy Environment,*

Stephen Macchia said, **"Conflict is cancerous to relationships if left unattended"**. Resolving organizational conflicts begins with an honest assessment of our heart in line with our personal values. Conflict across organizational functions and even basic interpersonal conflict is draining, time consuming, and painful. It does help to have a few skills to facilitate the mediation.

Value added organizations.

Every organization will benefit when the needs of its employees are regularly addressed. Apparently, customer satisfaction should be the bottom line, but employees will know when they are actually valued, and when priority is given to their concerns. It is the consultant's role to help shape and create a safe place and a sense of belonging for all employees. Management recognition of diversity issues makes a huge statement to everyone. This type of sensitivity heightens the awareness of all members and takes their mind-set off of themselves and turns it towards service. Sometimes, changing demographics in line with team leaders, and departments' signals that management embraces diversity, considers it as a priority, and is setting the tone for all employees.

The realization of the importance of diversity training at the workplace comes to penetrate the heart of all employees, and pulls every one along a common goal. The innovation, creativity, problem solving, cohesiveness, and brain trust in a heterogeneous work environment will be enhanced in a matter of time. As a "passionate" consultant, I long for organizations to reach out to all employees through their words and actions and say, "We need to remind ourselves, despite all our differences, just how much we share: common hopes, common dreams, and a bond that will not break." And, when that sentence becomes more than "politically correct," expressions printed in the policy book simply becomes a natural practice.

People side of consulting.

Consultants should ensure that the outcomes of their consulting meet the expectations of their clients, and are delivered on time and within cost. To succeed, the consultant must keep close eyes on the following:

   a. Organizational awareness – an ability to understand the environment and business pressures within the consulting assignment; read the organizational climate, understand the politics – the flow and pattern of it, and deal with diverse challenges and stakeholders' expectations.
   b. Team and interpersonal skills – consultants can rarely accomplish anything alone. We should be able to focus on both the task and relationship issues. We need management to foster a very open and supportive climate where employees are able to work without any ambiguity of their expected roles and responsibilities, and the need for management to realize the need to volunteer information and compassionate support when employees run into difficulties.

Consultants should also seize every agreeable trusting moment to change. Gail Sheehy says it well: "If we don't change, we don't grow. If we don't grow, we aren't really living."

I know you don't want to be distrustful as a "living-dead" manager – do you?

Exercises

   a. List and explain five factors causing distrust in organizations.
   b. Discuss five ways to fix the trust deficit syndrome.
   c. Is Organizational awareness important in business consulting? Why or why not?

d. Why is the "people side of consulting" important in achieving business success?
e. If conflict mediation skills are important, why do most consultants lack that skill? Suggest Five (5) ways consultants can develop conflict mediation skills for organizations.

Learning Agility – Leading Towards Your Best.

Learning Agility

Defined: ABILITY and WILLINGNESS to learn quickly, and then apply learned lessons to perform well in new and challenging leadership situations.

Learning agile leaders do the following:

- » Learn from experience – both successes and failures – and learn new things quickly.
- » Possess cognitive, attitudinal, and behavioral flexibility.
- » Continually grow, develop and evolve.
- » Interact more effectively.
- » Adapt well
- » Outperform peers
- » Promoted more frequently
- » Less likely to derail.

The most effective organizations and teams have the following core components:

- Mission

- Talent
- Norms
- Engagement
- Results

The most effective leaders intentionally focus on:

- **Task**
- **Thinking**
- **People**

As a leader, write down the percentage of time you spend on TASK, THINKING and PEOPLE to determine where you pay more attention.

High Performers and High Potentials.

High Performer: An employee, who is a key contributor, demonstrates high performance, is capable of lateral move, and may be qualified for a broader role within the same profession.

High Potential: An employee who has been identified as having a potential, ability and aspiration for successive leadership positions within the company. Often, these employees are provided with focused development as part of a succession plan.

Item	High Performance	High Potentials	Percentage
Percentage of high performers that are high potentials			29 percent

Percentage of high performers that are NOT high potentials			71 percent
Percentage of high potentials that are high performance			93 percent
Percentage of high potentials that are NOT high performers			7 percent

Source: High-potential management Survey, Corporate Leadership Survey.

From the table above, it is clear that a leader in an organization must concentrate on High Potentials instead of High Performers. This is the deductive reason:

    A. High Performers are NOT always High Potentials.
    B. High Potentials are Mostly High Performers.

The best predictor of future behavior/performance is _____ _____?

Or is it?

In similar situations → performance.

Different Situations → learning agility.

High performance may be a precondition to being identified as a high potential; learning agility is an overriding criterion for separating high potentials and non-high potentials.

Learning Agility Facets

Rate yourself on each of the facets using the following scale:

1= unsatisfactory   2 = inconsistent   3 = meet expectations
4 = highly effective   5 = exceptional

- ☐ **1. Interpersonal Acumen:** Understanding others and able to work well with a diverse group of people, instilling confidence, and engaging others constructively to accomplish organizational goals.

- ☐ **2. Cognitive Perspective**: Conceptualizing issues differently, examining problems from a high level, unique, and strategic perspective.

- ☐ **3. Environmental Mindfulness:** Being fully observant of one's environment, attentive to changing conditions and approaching in a nonjudgmental manner and regulating one's emotions effectively.

- ☐ **4. Drive to Excel:** Motivated by challenge, seeking difficult assignments, resourceful, and able to get things done.

- ☐ **5. Self-Insight**. Understanding oneself accurately, one's capabilities, weaknesses, beliefs, values, and personal goals.

- ☐ **6. Change Alacrity:** Curious, eager to learn, open-minded to new situations, and continually seeking innovative (at times risky) approaches to perform.

☐ **7. Feedback Responsiveness**: Actively soliciting and accepting feedback, contemplating its merits, and taking corrective actions.

- These seven learning agility facets are the results of the research of Dr. Ken De Meuse and are integral part of TALENTx7 Assessment.

The good news about Learning Agility is that we can practice and improve individual agility. All that leaders need to do is to determine how important these behaviors are to your organization.

Exercises

1. As a consultant, how would you improve your clients learning agility?
2. The most effective organizations and teams have the following core components:
   - Mission
   - Talent
   - Norms
   - Engagement
   - Results

How would you link all these core components together for effective and efficient organizational outcome?

3. The most effective leaders intentionally focus on:
   - Task
   - Thinking
   - People

What do you think is the best approach to focus on these three constructs to achieve the best results for organizations?

4. What was your score in the Learning Agility Facets assessment? Any surprises? What would you do to improve your score?
5. As a manager of an organization, would choose High Performers or High Potentials? Explain your positionality.

Interviewing Skills

Interviewing begins with resume and cover letter building. A great resume and cover letter speak for a job applicant until he/she is eventually interviewed. As an example, you apply for a good job that fits your skill set. However, as is the norm, there is the likelihood that about 20 other individuals will apply for the same job. The ratio of you getting this job then is 1:20. That means before the Human Resource calls you for phone interview or invite you for personal interview, only your resume and cover letter will be making a compelling argument for you to be hired.

Hiring and Development builds on recruiting and developing new employees that give an organization the chance to get more done, extend their reach, lighten their load and broaden their skills and capabilities (Abrams, 2010). The mechanics of adding a team member to the work family and various responsibilities will be analyzed in depth in order to understand personal development and growth.

Hiring your first employee is a big milestone on the road to becoming a 'real" company. Without employees, your growth is limited by how much efficient you can be in doing almost everything yourself and outsourcing the rest. Adding an employee gives you a chance to get more done, extend your reach, lighten your load and broaden the skills and capabilities of your enterprise.

Hiring employees is a wonderful opportunity for your own personal growth, and a unique chance to become the best boss your employees ever had. And when you become that boss, you'll discover that running a business (small or big), is even more rewarding, and more successful than before. When you hire an employee, you are adding a partner, a team member and a new member of your business "family."

Benefits of hiring new employees.

- Increased Success. When you hire a new employee, the motivate and existing employees to work harder. This leads to increased success.
- Quality of work-life increases, especially when existing workload is shared with the new employee.
- Stronger, smarter, and higher-achieving new employees mean a stronger company, who looks better than before.
- Quality of outcome could be ensured due to the new quality of employee.
- That means profit will increase and cost will be managed effectively.

Scope Out Your Specific Needs.

"The way a team plays as a whole determines its success. You may have the greatest bunch of individual stars in the world, but if they don't play together, the club won't be worth a dime." – Babe Truth.

You know you need help, and you're ready to take the step to hiring someone. Whoa! Before you run your first help wanted ad, you need to figure out a few things: what will your employee be doing, where will you put them, and can you afford to pay them.

Doing a bit of background work prepares you for the process of finding and hiring a great employee.

Example: You are a Hairdresser and Hiring Receptionist/Assistant.

You're hiring someone to do the support work to allow you concentrate on customers and earn more per hour on doing what you love – styling hair. The office assistant can answer the phone, shampoo waiting customers, clean and order supplies. The downside: they don't bring in direct, additional income. As you think of additional duties to share with the assistant, be aware of the two biggest mistakes business owners make when hiring an employee:

1. Handing over too much authority.
2. Not giving over any authority.

Recognize that you have to relinquish some control if you want your business to grow, and your employee to be effective and satisfied. You are almost certain to have a long list of things you'd like someone to do. Prioritize what you will like accomplished. Can they all be undertaken by the same person or you will need additional help?

Help Wanted, But How Much?

Now that you've decided what position you should fill, you need to consider how much time you'll require from an employee. Do you need:

- A. Full time employee (working 30-40 hours per week or more)?
- Part-time employee? Generally, part time workers are paid by the hour, and still covered by all employment laws.
- Independent contractors

Facts:

- Small businesses with 1 to 24 employees hire a quarter of their employees on a part-time basis.
- In businesses with more than 100 employees, part-timers make up only about 14 percent of the workforce.

(Source: Small Business Administration, 2016).

Deciding How Much Help You Need

Employee Type	Advantages	Disadvantages	Payroll Taxes	Quick Tips
Full Time	Larger labor pool to choose from; stability, loyalty & lower turnover.	More expensive, less flexible, higher benefits costs.	Yes	30-40 hours per week generally constitutes full-time status.
Part-time	Lower cost, greater flexibility, typically fewer benefits; still have direct supervision.	Likely increased turnover, harder to find professional/skilled staff; lower staff satisfaction	Yes	You pay the same percentage in employment taxes for part-time as full-time employees.
Independent Contractor	No employment taxes; great flexibility, experienced workers; no cost when not utilizing.	Higher per hour cost; may not be able to get them when you need them; not under your supervision.	No	Make sure you're following all IRS rules or face stiff penalties.

How Much Can You Afford?

- Review your current monthly cash flow.
- Estimate your current monthly profit.
- Estimate expected additional income.
- Estimate monthly taxes and benefits.

- Estimate any additional costs (energy, space, etc. from new hire)

INTERVIEWING SKILLS FOR A DREAM JOB

US Department of Labor, 2015

√ Marketing yourself to be hired
- Five percent jobs on the internet
- 24% through direct contact
- 23% through employment agencies.
- 48% through NETWORKING (referrals and word of mouth).

TIPS

√ Networking is information gathering on where you can contribute value to the organization.
√ Networking is all about giving
√ Create a profile from your resume in networking (11 seconds rule).
√ Join online networking site.
√ Look for opportunities to meet new people.
√ Volunteer
√ Attend trade association meetings.

Resume

√ Enhance Value, Strategy, Confidence, Open doors, and Interview Better.
√ <u>Top Three (3) Fixes of Resumes</u>
» Presentation
» Compelling
» Focus on results

Avoid/Use

Avoid	Use
I can	Achievements
I want	Reduced
I need	Increased
I require	Enhanced, Improved

Cover Letter

- ☐ Keep it short

Dear Robert:

I am applying for a position as a manager with your firm and know that I can produce extraordinary results.

I respect your time and know that my value, ability to contribute and past achievements are well documented on my attached resume. Thank you for your time.

Sincerely,

John Jones.

Remember!

- √ Excite and engage the employer.
- √ Cover letter should be part of the same file as the resume.
- √ Can send hard copy to them.
- √ Cover letter should recap your resume.

Interviewing Skills – Purpose

- √ Interviews allow both the employer and the job seeker to determine if there is a correct fit between them.
- √ First impressions can make a lasting impact for both the interviewer and the job seeker.

Interviewing Skills - Purpose

- ▶ Employers
    - √ Is the candidate qualified?
    - √ Are they a good fit for the company?
    - √ Determine of you are invited back for a second interview and ultimately whether you are offered a job.
- ▶ Job Seekers
    - √ Opportunity to meet and connect with the prospective employer.
    - √ Sell your skills and abilities.
    - √ Help you determine if you are a good fit for the company.

Interviewing Skills – Process

- ▶ Job Interview – 3 Step Process
    - √ Preparation
    - √ Presentation / The Interview
    - √ Post-Interview Follow Up

Process begins when you start sending out resumes/filling out applications and extends past the actual interview

Interviewing Skills – Preparation

- ▶ PREPARATION   - 1st Step
1. **Know yourself:**
    - √ Know your resume inside and out.

√ Be prepared to answer questions, give examples or tell a story about every job you have held and every achievement and education noted on the resume.
   √ Provide skills and strengths that you possess that are relevant to the job.
   √ Know your personal and professional goals and how they will fit with the company goals.
   √ BE TRUTHFUL. Don't exaggerate or give inaccurate, misleading information.

Interviewing Room – Sell Yourself!

▶ Three Hurdles
√ **On time (15 min).** Early? You rush them.
√ Firm handshake
√ Good eye contact and smile
√ Introduce yourself...I started in...
√ For the past 5 years, I have been...

Tips:

√ Keep your answer under a minute
√ Don't answer a question with a question
√ Be clear, edible, and concise
- **Que**: Where do you want to be the next 5 years?
- **Ans**: Sitting at your seat.
- **Turn all your past negative job experience into positive**
- Multitasker, how you resolve conflicts, use research of the company to your advantage, plan to resolve weaknesses, stay positive about past jobs and say you benefitted from their experience.

Why you get a Job?

√ Dress professionally and conservatively.

√ Leave your own style at the door and dress as the company requires.
√ Know your resume well.
√ Tell them about their company.
√ Give specific examples.
√ Bring passion to the room
√ Be professional and prepared.
√ Ask for business card for thank you note.:

Remember!

√ It takes just 2 minutes to get hired.
√ Most employers know in the first 2 minutes whether or not they will hire you (U.S. Department of Labor).

Interviewing Skills – Preparation

▶ PREPERATION
2. **Research Your Prospective Employer**
√ It is VITAL that you research the company, as well as the position for which you are applying.
√ Knowledge is power- it can help set you apart from the competition
√ In general, the higher the level or greater the responsibility of the position, the more extensive your research should be.

Areas to focus on:

1. General Information – Mission/vision, length of time in business, etc.
2. Key products and services – challenges and opportunities
3. Current issues / events – new developments, mergers, etc.
4. Major competitors
5. Organizational structure
6. Corporate Culture

Sources for Research:

√ Internet, Company webpage,
√ e-bulletin boards, blogs, Google searches, library,
√ professional trade associations, current employees

Interviewing Skills – Preparation

▶ PREPARATION
3. **Perfect an Elevator Speech**
√ Everybody engaged in a job search needs an Elevator Speech
√ Brief introduction that you always have ready when someone asks you, "So, tell me about yourself..."
√ Omit personal information. Should only contain job related information.
√ Write the speech and then practice it until it's second nature and you can deliver it smoothly and naturally without sounding overly rehearsed

Example of Elevator Speech

Karma R. Agnew, PHR

My interest in Human Resources started in College. I graduated Summa Cum Laude, number 3 in my class in only three years with a B.S. Degree in Business Management, with an emphasis in Human Resources. While in school, I completed two internships: one in Recruitment at Aflac and one in Employee Development at Kwik Trip. I have three years of experience in Human Resources Management, working in both the private and public as well as profit and not-for profit sectors. I am a generalist by trade and thoroughly enjoy the Employee Relations and Strategic Management aspects of the field. At this point, I am looking for a challenge in my career, focusing on facilitating strategic partnerships with senior leadership.

Another Example of Student Elevator Speech

I'm currently a Junior at Memorial High School and would like to continue my education after I graduate at Viterbo University, studying Nursing. I always knew I enjoyed taking care of people; I have been babysitting since I was 10 years old. Until I complete my schooling, I would like the chance to continue learning skills that will help me work with different people and improve my communication skills.

Interviewing Skills – Preparation

- ▶ PREPARATION
- 4. **Study the job description thoroughly and develop success stories from past jobs, achievements, and experiences**
- √ Behavioral interviews offer the perfect format for success stories
- √ Truthful tale that illustrates your skills and value to an employer
- √ Best success stories connect with the employer's needs and demonstrate that you have done it in the past and can do it again
- √ Provide the challenge/problem...action taken...result/resolution
- √ Include quantitative details.
- √ Understanding responsibilities required in the position will help you select the most appropriate stories to discuss
- √ Be SPECIFIC- answer with how you have handled this in the past- not "I would".

Interviewing Skills – Preparation

- ▶ PREPARATION
- 5. **Practice answering questions that may be asked during an interview**
- √ Practice – Practice – Practice

√ May make the difference between a good or poor interview and may ultimately result in whether or not you get the job

Interviewing Skills – Preparation

▶ PREPARATION
6. **Be prepared to ask questions of the interviewer**
√ Indicate your level of interest
√ General rule – ask 2 to 4 questions
√ Bring a list of questions to refer to, selecting the most relevant

Sample Questions to Ask:

√ What would you like to see accomplished in the position in the next 3 to 6 months?
√ How do you measure success in this position?
√ If I'm selected, what would be my 2 -3 highest priorities in the near future?
√ What would you identify as characteristics of a top performer in this position?
• **Don't ask about salary, benefits or time off until after a job offer has been made**

Interviewing Skills – Preparation

▶ PREPARATION
7. **Professional References**
√ Use professional references unless asked to provide personal references by the employer
√ Never use a reference unless you have obtained permission from them
√ Develop solid references that can speak with firsthand knowledge about your ability to perform the job.
√ Generally, you want to choose former supervisors, teachers, or ELITE team leaders.

√ Have accurate, up-to-date information for references, such as name, daytime phone, e-mail address and relationship to you.
√ You should have no less than 3 references

8. **Wardrobe and Grooming – You never get a second chance to make a first-impression.**
√ Simple truth- appearance matters.
√ Know the corporate culture (part of the research process).
√ General rule of thumb is to dress for the interview at a level that is one step above the position for which you are applying.
√ You may not need to dress this way once you get the job, but dressing appropriately for the interview is very important.
√ Be mindful of your breath. Carry mints with you.
√ Be careful of colognes, perfumes, lotions and aftershave. Use sparingly.
√ Review how you look both standing up and sitting down to ensure you look professional.

Wardrobe and Grooming Tips for Women.

√ Two-piece suit with skirt or pant or a dress is recommended. Solid blue, gray or black is best with neutral, solid color blouse.
√ Closed toed shoes or pumps are best. Make certain they are not scuffed and heels are not damaged. No Boots.
√ Hosiery should be neutral in color with no patterns. Make certain there are no runs. Carry an extra pair.
√ Jewelry: subtle and compliment your outfit, not distract from it.
√ Don't carry a briefcase and a purse- choose one.
√ Hair should be clean and neatly styled.
√ Light make-up and perfume.
√ Neatly manicured, clean nails.

Wardrobe and Grooming Tips for Men.

√ Solid color suit. Navy or dark grey.
√ Long sleeve shirt. White or solid color coordinated with suit.
√ Coordinating tie and belt.
√ Dark socks that coordinate with suit.
√ Leather shoes that are shined.
√ Neat, professional hairstyle.
√ Go conservative with jewelry; well-groomed beard and mustache if have them.
√ Neatly trimmed, clean nails.
√ Portfolio or briefcase.

What if I don't have a suit?

√ Dress slacks (or khakis) and a nice shirt are ok in most environments if a suit is not available.
√ Other guidelines still apply

What not to wear!

√ Jeans and tee shirts.
√ Shorts.
√ Casual sandals and tennis shoes
- **Remove facial piercings and cover tattoos.**
9. **Final Phase – 3 Important Things.**
  ▶ Know where you are going & how long it will take to get there.
    √ Do a practice run during the time you will be driving the route
    √ Know where and how long it will take to park & walk to building
    √ Always plan to arrive 15-20 minutes early
- **NEVER arrive to an interview late!**

Remember what to take with you.

√ Copies of your resume, completed application, reference sheet, copy of the job posting, directions to the destination, writing/note materials and other research materials you have accumulated

Interview Skills – Preparation.

▶ What not to bring to the Interview with you.
√ Friends, family members or children.
√ Cell phones- if you have them, turn them OFF.
√ iPod or any other electrical devices.
√ Food.
√ Drinks.
√ Cigarettes

Be prepared for the unexpected.

▶ Be polite and cordial to the receptionist.

PRESENTATION – 2ⁿᵈ Step

▶ Actual Interview.
  √ If you have done your research,
   • know the job position thoroughly and have practiced
   • you may be nervous but you will be much better prepared for questions that will be asked of you.
  √ Familiarize yourself with the different interview styles used by employers.
   • If possible, when scheduling the interview, try to obtain what type of interview will be conducted.
   • This will also help you to prepare for the interview.

Interviewing Skills – Presentation.

- ▶ Presentation - The first few minutes are crucial. Studies have shown that interviewers can form an overall impression within the first 2 minutes of the interview.
- ▶ Introduction TIPS:

√ Shake hands firmly with the interviewer. A firm hand shake is important and OFTEN mishandled.

√ While shaking hands, make good eye contact, smile and greet the person with "Pleased to meet you, I am…"

√ Be polite; use the formal address of Mr., Ms., Sir, Mom, etc. unless invited to do otherwise.

- ▶ Body Language.
    - √ Stand Tall.
    - √ Sit straight and tall and look attentive and enthusiastic.
    - √ Listen attentively but avoid staring at the interviewer.
    - √ Place all material you brought with on the floor beside you with the exception of a note pad.
    - √ Nod when appropriate to demonstrate interest and evidence that you are paying attention.
    - √ Remain calm; Don't fidget.
    - √ Be careful not to speak too quickly.
    - √ Respond to questions appropriately.
    - √ Be warm and conversational, but don't ramble.
    - √ Smile.

Interviewing Skills – Presentation

- ▶ Answering Questions.
    - • Sample Questions

√ Common Questions – Be careful, practice to "obvious" questions are often overlooked by job seekers and result in weak answers.

√ Can you tell me about yourself? Use the Elevator Speech.

√ Why do you want to work here?
   - • (do not reply with- I need a job)

√ What are your goals?
√ What are your strengths?
√ What experience do you have that's directly relevant to this position?
√ Why should we hire you?
√ What are your salary expectations?
√ What do you know about our company?

☐ Sample Questions

▶ Difficult Questions
√ What is your greatest weakness?
√ How would you describe your personality?
√ Have you ever been fired?
√ Why have you been out of work for such an extended period of time?
√ Have you ever had a disagreement with a coworker or your boss, and if so, how did you handle it? BE CAREFUL... never speak negatively of past or current jobs or employers.... Also- be honest... employers know people have disagreements!
√ What did you dislike most about your last job?
√ What was your biggest failure?

☐ Types of Interviews:

1. <u>Screening Interview</u> – Use of screening tools to ensure candidates meet the minimum qualifications.

May be conducted in the following formats.

√ Telephone Interview
√ Computer Interview
√ Videoconference

2. <u>One-on-One Interview</u> – Traditional interview
3. <u>Serial or Sequential Interview</u> - Candidates are passed from one interviewer to another throughout the course of the day. Sequential may last day, weeks or longer.
4. <u>Panel Interview</u> – Appear before a committee or panel of interviewers
5. <u>Group Interview</u> – Interview simultaneously with other candidates for the same position.

☐ Situation or Performance Interviews

1. <u>Audition Interview</u> – Candidate is put through a brief exercise or simulation to evaluate skills
2. <u>Stress Interview</u> – Intended to put the candidate under stress in order to assess their reactions under pressure or difficult situations

☐ Other Types of Interviews

1. <u>Informational Interviews</u> – Initiated by the job seeker. Informational interview without a reference to a job
2. <u>Mealtime</u> – Interview is conducted over a meal
3. <u>Follow Up Interviews</u>. This is where companies bring candidates back for additional interviews.

☐ Behavioral Interview - Many companies are increasingly using the behavioral interview.

√ Systematic process that ensures a fair selection process.
√ Use candidate's previous behavior as an indicator of future performance.
√ May involve standardized assessment instruments, such as personality, aptitude and interest inventories.
√ Involves directive and probing questions.

√ Questions may ask you to describe problem-solving skills, adaptability, leadership, conflict resolution, stress management, etc.
√ Involve what you thought, felt, did and the resulting outcome

☐ Behavioral Interview

▶ Competencies Assessed
√ Technical and professional skills and knowledge.
√ General skills / behavior - judgment, delegation, etc.
√ Personal Style - Adaptable, team player and so forth.
√ Motivations – Ongoing learning, independence etc.
▶ Answering questions in a Behavioral Interview
√ Be sure to include the following information in your answers.
√ Give a specific situation.
√ List the tasks/objectives that needed to be done.
√ The action you took.
√ The results / what happened

☐ Sample Behavioral Interview Questions.

√ Describe a time when two of the members of your team did not work well together? What did you do to get them to work together?
√ Give me an example of a project that best describes your organizational skills.
√ Tell me about a time when your work was criticized. How did you respond?
√ What is the most difficult decision you've had to make? How did you arrive at your decision? What was the result?

Interviewing Skills – Exercise.

▶ Answer Behavioral Question
- <u>S</u>--Gives a <u>S</u>pecific situation
- <u>T</u>--Contains the <u>t</u>asks/objectives that needed to be done
- <u>A</u>--The <u>a</u>ction(s) you took
- <u>R</u>--The <u>r</u>esults/outcome i.e. what happened

▶ Question: Have you ever had to deal with an upset customer? If so, what was it and how did you deal with it? What happened?

☐ Factors Rated by Employers During Interviews

1. <u>Education</u> – As it relates to the position
2. <u>Cognitive Abilities</u> – Judgment, logic, thought processes etc.
3. <u>Manner, Personal Traits</u> – Social poise, sense of humor, mannerism, self-confidence, listening skills etc.
4. <u>Appearance</u> – Grooming, Dress, Hygiene, Health
5. <u>Attitude</u> – Enthusiastic, outlook, willing to work hard, ability to accept criticism, interaction with work environment / people
6. <u>Level of Motivation</u> – Initiative, energetic, ambitious, goal oriented, accomplishments and achievements
7. <u>Leadership Qualities</u> – Mature, responsible, stable
8. <u>Interest</u> – Interest in position and company
9. <u>Overall Impression</u>

Interviewing Skills – Post Interview

▶ POST-INTERVIEW FOLLOW UP – 3rd Step.
▶ Thank you Notes.
√ Whatever the results of your interview, a follow up thank you note to the interviewer (s) is a nice gesture.
√ Can be a typed or hand-written letter or note. An e-mail is also acceptable. Customize the note.
√ Free of spelling or grammar errors.

√ Should be completed within 2-3 days of the interview.
√ Highlight key points you want to reiterate or forgot to say, information you learned about the company, express enthusiasm about the opportunity.
√ If you have decided that the position is not for you, it is perfectly appropriate to thank them for their time but respectfully ask that your name be removed from further consideration.

☐ POST-INTERVIEW FOLLOW UP

▶ Follow up to determine if decision has been reached
√ Hopefully you were given a timetable for the hiring decision. It is acceptable to ask this question.
√ Follow up at appropriate time to determine if a decision has been reached.
√ Opportunity to see if any further information is needed.
√ If past the deadline, send a letter or email expressing your continued interest. There may have been a delay in the decision.

☐ Self-Evaluation

√ Identify what went well in the interview.
√ Identify what did not go well in the interview.
√ Practice and continue to improve for the next interview
√ If you were not hired, it's not about you.

What Now?

▶ Review the STRUCTURED INTERVIEW PROCESS PACKET I have provided.
√ This will help to prepare you for your next interview.
√ Perfect your elevator speech.
√ Start thinking about what jobs you would be interested in.

Exercise

In the table below, you will find eight (8) myths of hiring. Your duty is to debunk those eight myths with the reality. Share the positive side of each myth with your knowledge of this week Module. On each myth, state what you think is real/right response should be.

In this post, you will provide reality for each myth.

Myth Versus Reality	
Myth	**Reality**
1. Hiring and employee costs too much money	
2. I must offer employees a whole range of costly benefits.	
3. I will have to pay payroll taxes as well as salary or wages.	
4. I do not have enough money saved up to hire full-time employees.	
5. I do not have enough space in my office for an employee.	
6. I will spend all my time on paperwork, managing payroll, and figuring taxes.	
7. Managing other people will take up too much of my time.	
8. Employees are lazy, more trouble than they're worth.	

2. Create your "Elevator Speech"
    a. Your Goal
    b. Your Experience that has prepared you to reach that goal
        1. i.e. Education
        2. i.e. Career Progression, School Projects, etc.

The Steward Leader

STEWARD LEADERSHIP IS a form of leadership which focuses on others, the community, and society at large rather than the self. A steward holds a position of trust and manages someone's property. That means the steward accounts for her services and understands she is just a caretaker of the position.

Here are some of the characteristics of steward leaders:

- Steward leaders adopt a "we" perspective instead of an "I" perspective.
- Steward leaders think about the long-term picture and make sure they are clear on what's important to the company's long-term success.
- Steward leaders understand that the company's core values (e.g. financial sustainability, product quality, ethical behavior) can be in conflict with personal values (e.g. money, recognition, prestige).
- Steward leaders align their work – and their decisions – with the organization's core values.
- Steward leaders consider the short term, but steadily work toward building a stronger team and aiming for better results in the longer term.

Steward leadership is contagious.

When employees see their managers behaving like stewards, they often adopt the same attitude. Stewardship encourages employees at all levels to adopt more pride in their work and take on tasks that are beyond their specified job duties. This mindset often leads to more innovation because steward leaders are more likely to come up with strategies that are more difficult to implement—like improving systems across departments or changing infrastructure.

Steward Leadership is rooted in faith: A protector of a house or guarding a house. The faith links the leader to a higher superior being, self, neighbor and other creation. A steward is a mere lessee of the property, money, relationships, talents, time, and even her life. That means all that she is and all the resources she leads (human and material) are not really hers to begin with. It means to manage everything to the best of our abilities for others glory, not our own empty glory.

The Steward Leader Model

From the Great Man theory (that leaders are born) through Strategic Leadership and beyond, the steward leader model stands apart in three ways:

a. Leadership Theories.
b. Begin with leadership acts deemed to be effective and try to work their way back to find common traits and characteristics.
c. Rely on the basic goodness of human nature as the basis for the work of leadership.
d. Have a common view that the leader moves people toward a goal of personal happiness with the hope and belief that people–and leaders–can actually know what makes them happy and can pursue it without harming their neighbor.

The steward leader approach is based on the transformation that takes place in the heart of the leader as a faithful and godly steward, and works from this inner transformation (which is ongoing) to the outward impact when a godly steward is called to lead. Steward Leadership answers "Who", not "How." Steward leaders empower their people, give away authority, value and involve others, seek the best in and from their people, and constantly lift others up, push others into the limelight and reward those who lead – all so that God's will may be done in a powerful way. Tony Blair (former British Prime Minister) on Leadership

"Leadership is not about being a normal human being – you are. As that mantle of responsibility floats by, it's despite your fear and despite your self-doubt and everything that you know could go wrong, you take the mantle and put it on." The stewardship matrix (Lyon, 2014) is below:

The Steward Leader Matrix

4 Levels of Transformation	Transformation in the Life of the Steward Leader	Trajectory in the Life of People He/She Leads	Trajectory in the Life of the Organization He/She Leads
Level One: Stewards of Our Relationship with God, Our Creator	The Steward Leader in the Presence of God	Steward Leaders are United with the People They Serve	Steward Leaders Cultivate Culture
Level Two: Stewards of Our Relationship with Our Self.	The Steward Leader in the Mirror	Steward Leaders Develop Whole People	Steward Leaders Harness the Power of People

4 Levels of Transformation	Transformation in the Life of the Steward Leader	Trajectory in the Life of People He/She Leads	Trajectory in the Life of the Organization He/She Leads
Level Three: Stewards of Our Relationships with Our Neighbors	The Steward Leader in Relationship	Steward Leaders Build and Value Community as its Own End	Steward Leaders are Caretakers of Their Community
Level Four: Stewards of Our Relationship with God's Creation	The Steward Leader in God's Creation	Steward Leaders Marshal Resources Effectively	Steward Leaders Create Organizational Consistency and Witness

Exercises

1. Reflect on what Steward Leadership is all about after reading these materials of the concept. Now, discussion this: **"WHAT DOES STEWARDSHIP MEAN TO YOU AND WHY?"** Please give practical example to support your ideas.

Based on your understanding of the topic of Steward Leadership, answer the following questions. Your response to each question must not exceed half of a page.

These are your questions:

2. As a steward leader, how are you united or intend to unite with the people you serve?

3. How do you cultivate or intend to cultivate a stewardship culture at your workplace?
4. How do you plan to develop "self" (yourself) and others at the workplace to be stewards?
5. How is your relationship with neighbors (as each one's keeper) and why?
6. How do you intend to build a community through stewardship and be a caretaker of your community?
7. How do you manage or intend to manage resources (both human and material) at work and why?

The Servant as Leader

WHILE SERVANT LEADERSHIP is a timeless concept, the phrase "servant leadership" was coined by Robert K. Greenleaf in The Servant as Leader, an essay that he first published in 1970. In that essay, Greenleaf said: "The servant-leader is servant first. It begins with the natural feeling that one wants to serve, to serve first. Then conscious choice brings one to aspire to lead. That person is sharply different from one who is leader first, perhaps because of the need to assuage an unusual power drive or to acquire material possessions.

The leader-first and the servant-first are two extreme types. Between them there are shadings and blends that are part of the infinite variety of human nature. "The difference manifests itself in the care taken by the servant-first to make sure that other people's highest priority needs are being served. The best test, and difficult to administer, is: Do those served grow as persons? Do they, while being served, become healthier, wiser, freer, more autonomous, more likely themselves to become servants? And, what is the effect on the least privileged in society? Will they benefit or at least not be further deprived? A servant-leader focuses primarily on the growth and well-being of people and the communities to which they belong. While traditional leadership generally involves the accumulation and exercise of power by one at the "top of the pyramid," servant leadership is different. The servant-leader shares power, puts the needs of others first and helps people develop and perform as highly as possible. However, servant leadership is problematic in hierarchical, autocratic cultures where managers and leaders are expected to make all the decisions. Here, servant leaders may struggle to earn respect.

Importance:

Remember that servant leadership is about focusing on other people's needs – **not** their feelings. Don't avoid making unpopular decisions or giving team members negative feedback when this is needed. Also, do not rely on it exclusively – use it alongside styles like Transformational Leadership, where you develop an inspiring vision of the future, motivate people to deliver this, manage its implementation, and build an ever-stronger team.

How to Become a Servant Leader.

According to Larry C. Spears, former president of the Robert K. Greenleaf Center for Servant Leadership, there are 10 important characteristics of a servant leader. These are:

1. Listening.
2. Empathy.
3. Healing.
4. Awareness.
5. Persuasion.
6. Conceptualization.
7. Foresight.
8. Stewardship.
9. Commitment to the growth of people.
10. Building community.

We realized that Servant Leadership paradigm have four constructs:

a. The leader is a steward.
b. The leader's mindset is centered on others.
c. The leader puts the needs of the led first.
d. The leader treats others as partners.

That means a servant leader **regards self as servant first, only assume a position as leader if and when it is the best way to serve, and in all of this puts the good of those led first without exploiting one's self.**

Exercise

1. What is the difference between a servant leader and a steward leader?
2. Which of the Spears 10 attributes of servant leadership can you relate to and why?
3. This is a reflection paper. Identify a hypothetical organization (it cold be a current organization or a future one; for profit or non-profit) that is using the Servant Leadership concept. Give a brief background of the selected organization, why they chose to implement Servant Leadership as a leadership model, and what the outcome was. Also, discuss any challenges you noticed or observed or positive lessons the organization learned along the way while implementing the servant leadership model. Your reflection must be five (5) pages. Your reflection will be graded based on the following: Introduction, Purpose of the reflection, Focus of your writing, Organization of thoughts, Evidence of knowledge of the concept of servant leadership, personal evaluation of the concept, convention (grammatical errors and mechanical accuracy) and a conclusion.

Power in Leadership

"Most powerful is he who has himself in his own power." - Seneca (5 BC - 65 AD).

For this ideation, we will look at the theory of power of leadership and explain how power manifests itself in leadership situations.

POWER IN HISTORY:

1. **Sophists of Ancient Greece.**
   √ Those with power had specialized knowledge; today's connotation from Plato who considered them greedy, and using rhetorical ambiguities of language in order to deceive others.

2. **German Sociologist Max Weber.**
   √ Charisma: Exceptional qualities; creates authority that arises out of devotion of followers (vs. tradition, legal precedent.) as sources of power.

3. **French & Raven's Five Sources of Personal Power.**
   √ Legitimate, reward, coercive, expert and referent power.

4. **Alvin Toffler's Power shift.**
   √ Three kinds of power: violence, wealth and knowledge.

5. **McClelland and Motivations.**
   √ Power comes from achievements and affiliations.

Studies of Leadership and Power.

a. Kanungo & Mendonca compared altruistic vs. egotistic leader's use of power.
b. Sashkins' book, ***Leadership That Matters,*** explains pro-social vs. personalized power (from McClelland) does leadership roles.
c. Joseph Nye's article talked about hard power (coercion) vs. soft power (attraction).

The Theory of Power in Leadership

Theory starts with a problem (e.g., Why do nations go to war?). Begin by thinking of a broad problem related to power in an organizational leadership context. Then write a simple, researchable question on that problem.

Next, posit a "theory of power in leadership" that could be tested in in a new context. What data would you need to collect for that? You don't need to have a hypothesis written, but you might consider such statements to guide your discussion.

This is only for our discussion in thinking through what theory is and how we might explain how power manifests itself in leadership situations.

A Few Classical Understanding of Power.

Power has many meanings, most of which imply (a capacity for) control or force and may refer to:

- Power (physics) is the amount work done or energy transferred per unit of time. The term might be confused with Force (physics), which has a different definition and meaning.
- Electric power generation is the process of converting any form of energy to electrical energy. E.g. power station, nuclear power, solar power, wind power or geothermal power.
- Optical power of a lens is the inverse of its focal length.
- Statistical power is the probability that a statistical test will reject a false null hypothesis.
- In social sciences, Power (sociology) is the ability to make choices or influence outcomes, which is also power held by a person or a group of people in a society.
- Political power is power held by a person or group in a country's political system.
- Reserve power is power exercised by a head of state in certain exceptional circumstances.
- Power in international relations is the ability of national states to influence or control other states, which may be distinguished as Historical Power, Middle Power, Regional Power, Great Power, Super Power or Hyper Power.
- Economic Power has no agreed-upon definition. it could mean purchasing power of goods and service of a given country or monopoly power, the ability to set prices of goods and services.
- Will Power, is a prominent concept in the philosophy of Friedrich Nietzsche.
- In law, we have legal power, constitutional power, judicial power or executive power.

- In movies, we have power (film), a 1968 film based on the novel.
- In music, we have power ballad, a song genre. We also have Power Noise, a sub-genre of heavy metal music.
- In literature, we have The Power Novel, a 1956 novel by Frank M. Robinson and the 48 laws of Power book by Robert Green (I recommend Green book for your reading pleasure on this topic if you have the resources to buy it).

Exercises

a. Mention a leader who has used his/her power of leadership positively to influence society (this leader should be different from the one you chose for your discussion).
b. Give a brief background of the leader, the kind of power the leader has (e.g. knowledge power, charisma, achievement, affiliation, coercive, referent, expert, legitimate, etc.).
c. Special things he/she did that was exceptional.
d. Suggest lessons those aspiring to be leaders may learn from the leader you selected.
e. How you will personally implement some of the chosen leader's ideas at your current workplace.

Your response must be three pages (excluding cover page). It must follow the prompt, have an introduction, detailed analysis, conclusion, and sources cited. There should be no errors.

Measuring Leadership Performance Through Coaching

The ability to raise the performance of your employees and seek long-term goals for them to work toward is an important element of being a good leader. Through coaching, you can develop employees to take on more responsibilities and give yourself more time to get on with the job of leadership. Coaching successfully will help you get the best from your team and let you focus on achieving better results for your organization.

- Understand coaching
- Use coaching to develop skills and talents in their work teams.

Coaching helps leaders bring out potentials of their team. Leaders use it to deal with immediate problems, as a constructive way to interact with their staff, and as an aid to their long-term organizational development.

So, what is coaching?

Coaching is the art of improving the performance of others. Leaders who coach encourage their teams to learn from and be

challenged by their work. Create the conditions for continuous development by helping your team to define and achieve goals.

How Coaching Works!

The coaching process closes the gap between an individual's or team's present level of performance and the desired one. This can happen within a single coaching session, or over a long cycle of sessions. As a coach, you will help develop your employees by mutually assessing performance, discussing the present situation, defining achievable goals, exploring new initiatives, and supporting a coachee in their plan of action.

The Coaching Process is below:

1. **Definition** (Determining performance goals).
2. **Analysis** (Understand the present reality).
3. **Exploration** (Explore options to achieve goals).
4. **Action** (Say when tasks will be done).
5. **Learning** (Implement agreed upon actions)
6. **Feedback** (Review progress at next session).

Points to Remember:

- If your team has a positive attitude, it is more able to face new challenges in the coaching process.
- A good coach encourages a team to discuss their ideas.
- Employees should have the necessary resources to achieve their goals.
- Use coaching to develop skills and talents in your team.
- Encourage employees to come to their own conclusions.

The Difference between Coaching and Mentoring.

- In this session Alysia Clary, in a YouTube 5.34 minutes video discusses:

a. The differences between coaching and mentoring.
b. Developing coaching and mentoring strategies that eliminate undesirable workplace behaviors.
c. Developing methods that increase the quality of feedback in organizations.
d. Designing systems that ensure timely and meaningful communication in organizations.
e. Formulating techniques to improve individual performance.

The link is below:

- https://www.youtube.com/watch?v=tWaNC1jvaIY

Involving People.

- Teams in business need high morale to perform well. Research shows that when people take part in decision making they have greater commitment to the final decision making.
- Find out what your team values most in its work.
- Agree on clear performance standards so that the team has a level against which to assess itself.

Exercises

1. Analyze four ways management can involve the people in their organization to perform better.
2. Examine four differences between coaching and mentoring.
3. Explain the coaching process, the way you understand it and how you will use the steps involved in achieving organizational success.
4. Point out three ways leadership performances can be measured through coaching.

A New View of Life and Work for Leaders

A NEW VIEW of Work Creates New Goals and Action Plans for Leaders (Northouse, 2010). Change has impacted every aspect of doing business. As organizations reshape themselves to survive and compete in a global economy, new rules, new lifestyles, and new modes of communication have combined to create a much different environment from that of yesterday. The drastically changing world of work requires both organizations and leaders to transform themselves; to redefine the way work is organized and performed. In order to do this, leaders must first understand what the change is that they are dealing with, and why it is happening. Then, they can acknowledge and accept this change by shifting their attitudes and thinking. With this insight, you will be able to create new goals and take new actions as a leader for your organization

Business is in a State of Perpetual Change. Organizations and individuals must become fast, fluid, flexible, friendly and adaptable if they are to survive and thrive in today's fast-paced business environment. The following external forces are demanding that organizations and individuals change the very nature of how work will be done.

- Globalization
- Emerging technology
- Changing markets
- Corporate mergers & acquisitions
- Workforce Development

* Quality initiatives.
* Streamlining.
* Restructuring
* Revitalization.
* Re-engineering

Paradigms.

Sometimes, individual leaders can't change the situations, but they can manage their responses to it. These responses are often defined by the leader's perception of the situation, or PARADIGMS. Paradigms are set of rules and regulations we use to define our boundaries and provide rules for success. Paradigms play a critical role in the effectiveness and success of career planning as well. In order for you to do things differently, or do different things, you must think differently about yourself, your work and your work environments. The fundamental shift in thinking that needs to take place involves the "unspoken Employment Contract." We need to let go of the traditional paradigms and create and embrace new ones.

Traditional Paradigms → Evolving Paradigms

√ A shift is not about EITHER/OR, but BOTH and MORE.
√ By dropping your boundaries in thinking around the traditional paradigms to perhaps include some of the evolving paradigms, you are able to create more options for yourself.

Changing Paradigms in the Workplace

Traditional	Evolving
Job	Work
Permanent structure	Fluid structure
Manager	Customer, client, leader.
Employee	Vendor
Salary, benefits	Fees
False security	Personal control
Entitlement	Marketability

Changing Paradigms in the Workplace

Traditional	Evolving
Loyalty to company	Commitment to self, work.
Employment	Employability
Job descriptions, titles.	Skill sets, competencies.
Career ladder	Career lattice
One career	Portfolio career

Differences

Traditional Employees are likely to:	Emerging Employees are more likely to:
1. Demand long-term job security from their employer.	1. Reject job security as a driver of commitment.
2. Believe employers are responsible for career growth	2. Take personal responsibility for career growth.
3. Be less satisfied with their jobs.	3. Be more satisfied with their jobs.
4. Believe changing jobs often is damaging to career.	4. Believe changing jobs often is part of growth within their organization.
5. Define loyalty as tenure.	5. Define loyalty as accomplishment.
6. View work as an opportunity for income only.	6. View work and view job assignments as a chance to grow.

Identifying Your Paradigms

"We will need to learn a whole new way of getting work done. We will need to develop new attitudes towards employment, new expectations regarding security, new ideas about career, and new habits to succeed under these circumstances." – William Bridges.

Paradigms can create boundaries or barriers. When you think about setting new career goals and exploring career interests, perhaps some barriers (paradigms) immediately come up and you think, "I can't/wont..."

For example:

- I can't spend the time in a weekend course to explore a new career interest because I am busy.
- I shouldn't have to market myself. I've been in this career/job for 20 years. My credentials speak for themselves.
- I can't do other work or additional responsibilities. It is not in my job description.

Research Findings.

According to a recent study published by the ***American Sociological Review***, 70% of American workers struggle with finding a work-life system that works for them. For many in the workforce, achieving any type of work-life balance can seem like a myth, especially when technology has made us accessible around the clock. Time free from workplace obligations seems to become ever more elusive. Despite these realities, there are those that have managed to have carved out satisfying and meaningful lives outside of their work. Here are some of the tools they practice:

They Make Deliberate Choices About What They Want in Life.

Instead of just letting life happen, people who achieve work-life balance make deliberate choices about what they want from life and how they want to spend their time. They talk to their partners, spouses, and others who are important in their lives, and come up with a road map of what is important to them, how they want to spend their time and commit to following their path.

They Regularly Communicate About What's Working and What Isn't.

Work-life balance going off the rails is usually a result of letting things slide as opposed to any kind of intentional choice. People who are good at staying on track make a conscious choice to continually talk to the important people in their lives about what is working or not, and make decisions to change direction if needed. While life happens and situations change, they avoid ending up in a place they didn't want to be due to drifting along.

They Set Aside Time for Family, Friends And Important Interests.

People who have managed to carve out a work-life balance that works for them don't just wait to see what time is left over after work. They make a point of planning and booking time off to spend outside of work and powerfully guard this time. While emergencies happen and situations come up that need their attention at work on occasion, they strongly resist any intrusion on this time.

They Set Their Own Parameters Around Success.

People who manage work-life balance have developed a strong sense of who they are, their values, and what is important to them. Using this as a guideline for everything they do helps them determine what success means to them. They know what makes them happy and strive to get more of that in their lives. While their time may be seen by others as being skewed towards either work or life, it is what they consider balanced that works for them.

They Turn off Distractions.

People who maintain balance are able to turn off their electronic devices to enjoy quality uninterrupted time doing matters they enjoy. They realize that multitasking is a myth and focus on the task at hand. Having developed the ability to compartmentalize their time, they seek out moments to simply enjoy the experience and savor life. Often, they have discovered meditation, music, physical activity, or some other interest that allows them to get away from the pressures of everyday life to relax, rejuvenate, and regenerate themselves.

They Have Goals Aligned with Pursuing Their Passion.

Many people go through life and get caught up in situations and circumstances that end up controlling them. Those that achieve balance have a defined plan around time frames and are willing to make some sacrifices to get what they want in the end. For example, many entrepreneurs typically plan to spend a substantial amount of time in the early part of their businesses. Those that achieve balance down the road see this as a sacrifice that will allow them to spend extra time and energy in other areas they are passionate about once the business is established.

They Have Developed A Strong Support Network.

People who have achieved good balance have a strong support network they can depend upon to help them get through difficult times. They are givers who typically extend themselves to help out in their family circles and communities. They tend to have a variety of interests and are always open to new learning and possibilities. They are curious, open, and want to experience life to the fullest.

How Millennials View Work-Life Balance

- **Long-term:** Millennials aren't driven by the thought of working hard for the next 40 years and then retiring. Rather, they are driven by the idea of building a life and career that can withstand the continuous reinventions and pivots that their long-term careers in the 21st century will require.
- **Integrated:** Millennials are more interested in leveraging today's tech to integrate work and life versus just balancing them. The term "work-life balance" implies that work is separate from life, but in reality, it's all life. Forcing people to put work and life into separate boxes that never overlap is unrealistic in today's always-on world.
- **Engaged:** Millennials view work-life balance as being fully engaged with the task, activity, or people they are currently involved with. Work-life balance isn't necessarily about physical time and place, but it is about the state of mind and mental margin that Millennials experience. (Some Millennials may need help from leaders to turn off the distractions to ensure they can be fully present in order to maximize a balance.)
- **Fluid:** Millennials want the work-life balance to be fluid, free, and flexible to prioritize whatever (work or life) is most important that day. To them, work-life balance means not having rigid boundaries between work and life. A more fluid approach ensures less stress.

- **Personal:** Millennials want all aspects of their professional and personal lives to receive the same level of attention, priority, and progress. They want a healthy mix of achieving professional goals and time to pursue personal goals. A sense of freedom and flexibility to be fulfilled and supported in both their personal and professional endeavors is critical. An example might be traveling for work and then staying an extra day to explore the area (while remaining available to be reached for work-related items that come up)or doing what needs to be done at work and then attending a child's school function later that day.

To Millennials, work-life balance is about what matters most to them as individuals and taking the steps to achieve it.

Additional Resources: Steven Covey in his book, The 7 Habits of Highly Successful People has a powerful analogy for how Millennials should view work-life balance:

Stop thinking your life needs to be "balanced." Balance implies things need to be of equal relation in order to reach success. I believe your life from birth to death should be thought of as a symphony. A great symphony is played with many different types of instruments and each played at different levels of intensity at different times during the performance. Sometimes you need to play the drums really hard or a flute really soft. Your commitments, just like instruments in a symphony, need to be adjusted to whatever is most important at that point in time. The goal is not to have work-life balance. It is to have work-life harmony.

Dan Thurmon, author of "Off Balance on Purpose: Embrace Uncertainty and Create a Life you want" said, "The perpetual quest for balance ends up limiting growth, progress, and the quality of life." Thurmon suggested that perfect balance is unachievable and, upon closer inspection, undesirable. We must be open to forcing ourselves off balance on purpose when we need to give an area of life more attention.

Exercise

1. In the table below, list five Traditional and Five Evolving paradigms different from the one you have learned.

Traditional	Evolving
1.	1.
2.	2.
3.	3.
4.	4.
5.	5.

Identifying barriers in shifting your paradigms.

Part I: Identify "Barriers."

Identify those "I can't/I won't" barriers in your career that always seem to echo in your mind. It may be helpful to refer to ideas from this chapter.

1. _____

2. _____

3. _____

Shifting Paradigm

Part II: Shifting your paradigm

Now try to shift your paradigms by restating, or re-framing your "**I/Can't I/won't**" statements. State a negative paradigm and restate the statements into a positive one.

For example:

Negative: I can't spend the time on a weekend course to explore a new career interest, because I am too busy.

Restated Positively: I am proactive about my career.

Negative: I can't take responsibility for my own employability and keep my skills up to date.

Restated Positively: I leverage my skills to support my company's business objectives.

Your exercise: State a negative statement and shift your paradigm in a Restated Positive Statement as given in the example above.

1. Negative:

    1. Restated Positively:

2. Negative:

    1. Restated Positively:

3. Negative:

    1. Restated Positively:

Develop Your Change Management Goals.

Directions:

You are now ready to create preliminary career/change management goals. How do you see yourself behaving, the tasks you will be doing, your attitude, what will be different, etc.?

Examples of Goals:

- To create more flexible work options.
- To define and develop my portfolio of skills to market internally and externally.
- To keep informed and up-to-date on trends in my industry.

My GOAL Is..._____

Objective Setting.

Directions:

Take your goal from the previous exercise and jot down three (3) realistic and desired outcomes of your goal.

1. _____

2. _____

3. _____

Action Plan

Directions:

Choose an objective from the previous exercise and describe the actions/steps that will enable you to achieve your objective. Your responses must match your action period. For example, if your action period is One Month, who needs to be involved and how, likely obstacles, how you will handle obstacles, and results you expect must match your One Month Action Plan period. (

ACTIONS COULD TAKE: (Choose one...24 hours, One Week or One Month)

24 hours:

One Week:

One month:

Who Needs to be Involved and How?

Likely Obstacles I Anticipate:

How I will handle the Obstacles:

Results I Expect:

Judgment on the Job

Good judgment in leadership is the ability to make considered decisions or come to sensible conclusions based on information available to the leader at a certain time period (Highouse, 2002).

The focus here is on: (a) Identifying scenarios at the workplace and make the appropriate judgment, and (b) Applying leadership development models in making appropriate judgment at work situations. **Technical skills alone do not ensure success on the job.** The ability to apply good judgment is critical today in leadership, more than ever.

Before we Dig into Good Judgment, A Look at Leadership Development.

Be sure to answer the critical questions in Leadership Development below:

a. Who defines you?
b. What or who is your reference point of validating your contributions and purpose?
c. What does it mean to be effective as a leader?
d. Are individuals capable of expanding their capacity to learn and lead?
e. What constitutes an effective leadership experience?

f. What are the critical factors in stimulating personal leader development?

Leadership Development Comes from Being Authentic to Self: Authenticity.

If we lead out of who we are, then it is important to know who are we.

Authenticity involves both owning one's personal experience (values, thoughts, emotions, and beliefs) and acting in accordance with one's true self (expressing what you really believe and behaving accordingly (Gardner, Avolio, Luthans, May & Walumba, 2005). Authentic leaders are "those who are deeply aware of how they think and behave and are perceived by others as being aware of their own and others' values/moral perspectives, knowledge, and strengths; aware of the context in which they operate; and who are confident, hopeful, optimistic resilient, and high moral character. The concept of authenticity extends beyond the authenticity of the leader as a person to encompass authentic relations with followers and associates and characterized by:

a. Transparency, openness and trust.
b. Guidance toward worthy objectives, and
c. An emphasis on follower development.

Components of Authentic Leadership.

- Self-awareness. Understanding self and its impact on others.
- Internalized moral perspective: Behavior guided by internal moral standards/values.
- Balanced processing: Open to, inviting of, and objective about others opinions.

- Relational transparency: Open and honest about presenting one's true self, both positive and negative. (Northouse, 2010, p. 216-218).

Leader and Leadership Development in Authenticity.

"Leader" development is the expansion of a person's capacity to be effective in leadership roles and processes. "Leadership" development, on the other hand, is the expansion of the organization's capacity to enact the basic leadership tasks needed for collective work: setting direction, creating alignment, and maintaining commitment (Velsor, McCauley and Ruderman (2010).

Leadership Development Model: Assessment

Assessment:

- Assessment provides an individual with a baseline understanding of current strengths, levels of performance and effectiveness, and primary development needs.
- It clarifies the "gap" between current and preferred state.

Leader Development Model

Challenges:

- In order for development to take place, individuals must be forced into new experiences which call into question:

a. The adequacy of skills, capacities and approaches.
b. Habitual ways of thinking and acting.
c. Well-worn assumptions, beliefs, sense-making.
d. Existing strengths and preferences.

Thomas Malcom Muggeridge, former English Journalist and Satirist on Hardships

"Contrary to what might be expected, I look back on experiences that at the time seemed especially desolating and painful with particular satisfaction. Indeed, I can say with complete truthfulness that everything I have learned in my seventy-five years in this world, everything that has truly enhanced and enlightened my existence, has been through affliction and not through happiness, whether pursued or attained." – Malcom Muggeridge.

Leader Development Model: Support.

Support:

- The element of support provides a safe holding environment during a "challenge" experience.
- Clarification and confirmation of learning is offered, and renewed sense of confidence is one's ability to learn and grow is fostered.

The Developmental Process: Personal factors that influence leader's growth:

a. Acceptance of responsibility for personal growth.
b. Understanding of personal preferences that "get in the way" of intentional engaging in new experiences.
c. Recognition of when new approaches are required.
d. Willingness to go "against the grain" of comfort.
e. Frequency of reflection upon what and how one is learning.
f. Commitment to persistence against setbacks.
g. Employ a variety of learning strategies to expand capacity.

The Developmental Process: **Leader Growth Conspirators**

a. Doing what one knows how to do well.

b. Doing what is working well at the present.
c. Avoiding the discomfort, anxiety, and risk associated with personal growth.
d. Preference for performance over learning.
e. Personality preferences.
f. Low and high self-esteem (self-efficacy.)

Reflective Questions for Getting Unstuck.

1. Am I going against the grain of my learning history?
2. Am I tackling the issues that I have historically avoided?
3. Am I using new processes that I committed to, or am I falling back on methods that are already within my comfort zone?
4. Am I getting stuck in same patterns that usually traps me?

What develops in leader development?

Self-Management Capabilities

- Self-awareness.
- Ability to balance conflicting demands
- Ability to learn
- Leadership values.

What develops in leader development?

Social Capabilities.

- Ability to build and maintain relationships.
- Ability to build effective work groups.
- Communication skills.
- Ability to develop others.

What develops in leader development?

Work Facilitation Capabilities.

- ❀ Management skills
- ❀ Ability to think and act strategically
- ❀ Ability to think creatively
- ❀ Ability to initiate and implement change.

NOW, Back to Applying Good Judgment on the Job. Apply all the knowledge of Leader and Leadership Development. Apply knowledge of Authentic Leadership.

Related Quotes of Identifying and Applying Good Judgment on the Job.

"We don't receive wisdom; we must discover it for ourselves after a journey that no one can take for us or spare us." – Marcel Proust, French Novelist, 1871-1922.

"Wisdom: I often regret that I have spoken; Never that I have been silent." – Publilus Syrus.

Good Judgment may be said to be made up of:

√ Experience.
√ Character.
√ Curiosity.
- ▶ Experience allows us to see the rewards and consequences of our behavior as well as that of others.
- ▶ Our Character serves as guidance – a moral compass – to help us determine when something is important and within what personal boundaries we will choose to respond.
- ▶ Curiosity is part of when we know we are never finished learning.

Contrary to popular belief, judgment is *not* a negative behavior. Every piece of stimulus that comes into our life experience—be that a new person, a new taste, or a new sensation—is filtered through our belief system. After the belief passes through the filter, we have a judgment. In its simplest form, this judgement tells us either we like something or we don't. This process is like our own GPS for decision-making. Why then, does choice sometimes seem so complicated?

Why Judgment Is Complicated

1. **Quick logic vs. slow logic.** There are two entirely different ways that this filter process can happen. The first—quick logic—happens in a millisecond. An example of this would be pulling your hand away from a hot burner before you even feel the burn. This type of processing happens without a conscious thought process that weighs the pros and cons of pulling your hand away.

   The second is slow logic. An example of this would be if a senior high school student is admitted into two colleges and needs to choose one. They might make a list of pros and cons for each, including things like cost, location, and possible majors. After careful deliberation, they would make a calculated choice. This is also a judgment. Any time you choose one thing over another, you are judging one thing or opportunity as better for you than another.

   A study by Daniel Kahneman, psychologist and author of **Thinking Fast, Thinking Slow**, shows that choices made using quick logic are our better choices.

2. **Analysis paralysis.** Research is a valuable tool to make informed decisions, but sometimes having too much information leads us to analysis paralysis. It's a fact of our nature that we often want to be "right" in our decisions. Recognizing that sometimes there is not a right choice or a perfect choice, just the best solution for now can

be helpful. Also realizing that decisions are timely. Set a deadline and stick to it for big decisions. You can also practice this with little decisions. When you go out to eat at a restaurant, decide that you will settle on your first choice and stick to it. Close the menu and move on.
3. **Popularity vs. Individuality.** The third reason we might try not to judge is sometimes our **internal GPS** doesn't align with popular opinion. When this occurs, sometimes we question our own ideas, or even if we feel confident in our judgment, we can hesitate to share it with someone who doesn't agree. Our need for harmony can cause us to shush our inner voice. This is a habit that will eventually lead your inner voice to whisper to you rather than speak confidently.

Five Ways to Improve Your Judgment

In the words of 19th-century writer Henry James, "I intend to judge all things for myself; to judge wrongly, I think, is more honorable than to not judge at all."

1. **Remind yourself** of times that your judgment served you well. This fuels confidence in your ability to trust yourself.
2. **Avoid flip-flopping** once you have decided or made judgment. If your gut tells you to try a vegetarian diet, don't allow external opinions or difficulty in changing your lifestyle to be an excuse for you to not follow your gut.
3. **Practice on little things** like clothing choice and menu options so that when bigger judgment calls need to be made, you have evidence to support your belief that you are good at this.
4. **Never judge someone as less to make yourself feel like more**. Knowing who you are and being confident about it lessens the feelings of comparison that might lead us to judge someone.

5. **Meditate.** Time spent in meditation leads to a sort of shaking up of our thought patterns and beliefs. This allows us to escape from the patterns and examine them. When you spend more time being mindful of your habits and thoughts, you begin to notice a shift in how judgments work for you.

How to Have Better Judgment at Work (A personal experience of a Leader at a conference)

1. Don't Zone Out

The most inexcusable part about my "situation" (as we will now refer to it) was I didn't even remember my thought process. I couldn't justify my actions. Why? Because I was "in the zone." Or rather, I was zoned out. I was doing my thing, the monotonous daily tasks I had come to take for granted. My brain was on autopilot. I ran hundreds of transactions a day. At some point, it only makes sense I'd stop paying close attention to each one

Good judgment is an active process. Engage the brain. If you feel yourself falling into a mindless routine, shake it up. Start working with the opposite hand or move the items you use most frequently. Showing strong judgment doesn't mean you won't ever make mistakes, but when you do, you should have a clear understanding (and recollection) of what thought process led you to that conclusion.

Slow Down

The truth is, I was probably competing with the other tellers to see who could move through customers the fastest. Man, I hate admitting this. But that was a common occurrence. I was a manager so running a teller drawer wasn't my favorite thing to do. I only jumped up to help out when the line was out of control. And my presence always forced the other tellers to pick up the pace. We made it a game as a way to relieve the tension. That backfired.

Never sacrifice quality for speed. It's so tempting, especially when impatient customers are right in front of you. But breathe deep and take slow, methodical action. Good judgment requires time. Give yourself a minute to think about what you're doing. Rushed decisions are never as defensible as those made with measured, deliberate consideration.

Realize Multitasking Is Dangerous

You guessed it. I was multitasking. It might not seem like it at first, but my attention was in fact divided. I was running a transaction while chatting it up with a customer. Now, I'm not saying I should have ignored the man in front of me.

But there's a time to shut up and focus, which I never did. I was more concerned with being friendly. I probably was trying to up-sell him to an investment product. I definitely wasn't giving the most important task in front of me the attention it deserved.

I've written before about the dangers of multitasking so I won't rehash my point-of-view here. Just remember: Good judgment requires full focus. Give it less and you'll get less.

Realize Stress Manipulates

It's only been in the last few years I've learned how to appropriately manage my stress. Before that, I truly let it run wild. Stress has a way of manipulating your thoughts. Scientifically, it can actually alter your brain chemistry. Stress can physically change the way you see the world and how you react to it. If you're under severe stress, you can pretty much guarantee your judgment will suffer. Get it under control now or pay later.

Realize People Aren't All As Nice As You

This is a hard lesson to learn. I worked at the bank right after college and, until that point, I didn't really understand just how much "bad stuff" happened each day out in the big world. Don't get me wrong—I wasn't an idiot. But I always thought I could SEE danger. And I trusted my gut.

So, I figured danger would either jump out with a neon sign over its head or I'd instinctively just know. Turns out, danger hides in all kinds of charming, fun, easy-to-talk-to places. Danger lives inside the most unsuspecting people and moments.

Good judgment means you're willing to see what's really there, even when it's hard. You're willing to look beneath the surface and confront the reality—that people aren't always good and truthful. You may be a target. You may be the person who looks easily swayed or distracted, the one whose judgment looks questionable. Don't let them get away with it. Show them your judgment is sharp and nothing gets by you.

I wonder what it would have been like if I had followed these tips on that fateful day. Would I have stopped the man? Would I have notified the police, saved the bank thousands of dollars, and possibly even played a central role in bringing down the fraud ring this man was a part of? Who knows? It'll always be a question for me.

Exercise

1. Share experience of a time at work when you used poor judgment, learned from the experience, and later were able to apply good judgment in a similar situation (One-page response).
2. Good judgment is not something we are born with...it is something we are continuously learning.

In what aspects of your work are you confident that you will apply good judgment now? (Your Strengths)	In what aspects of your work would you like to be able to apply good judgment (Areas you'll like to develop or improve)
1.	1.
2.	2.
3.	3.
4.	4.
5.	5.

State and explain what good judgment in the following scenarios is:

a. Frank takes credit for the work others do. He seems to be in the spotlight all the time. When your manager notices something has been done, Frank takes credit for it immediately. It really makes some people angry. They don't always want to be saying to the manager 'I did that, not Frank." Frank has a way of making it sound like he does all the work and you and others just stand watching him (Half a page response).

b. Ann is new to the team and has just completed her training program. As her cubicle is near yours, you overhear her speaking with customers in a way that you know is making them angry. She is short with them and tends to argue in most of the conversations you are hearing. You know this is the opposite of what she learned in the training, but you are not her manager, nor did you train her. (Half a page response).

c. Your team hired a new member, John, from a competitor company. Your manager is hoping to learn something about how the competition is positioning their products so successfully in the marketplace. A couple weeks after John came on board, you and John were both in the copy room making copies. While chatting casually, you notice that he is copying company confidential product specs from his old company. (Half a page response).

d. Your manager seems to have real trouble making decisions. She avoids meetings where decisions are on the agenda and she is often busy in her office with the door shut when you want to get the OK to proceed on something requiring her authority. When you do catch her, she says, "You use your own good judgment." (Half a page response).

International Negotiations

NEGOTIATION IS THE art and science of securing agreements between two or more parties (Katz, 2006). It is a skill that is central to all occupations and one that is used every single day. Negotiation is a skill that is critical to your success whether you are:

- Dealing with a highly political and emotionally charged situation
- Determining the price and terms when acquiring or selling products or services
- Allocating or requesting project resources for your teams
- Championing a new initiative for your company
- Navigating the political minefields of your firm
- Forming alliances or joint ventures with external partners

International negotiation is defined as a process of power-based and skilled-based dialogue intended to achieve certain goals or ends, and which may or may not thoroughly resolve a particular dispute or disputes to the satisfaction of all parties. That means international negotiation is both a science and skill and have different expectations than negotiating locally.

Two things to watch for in international negotiations are: (a) Language, and (b) Nonverbal behaviors.

- √ Meet Al-Ajeib Manager in Doha, Qatar.
- √ First meeting
- √ Keeps you waiting for 45 minutes
- √ Polite but reserved welcome
- √ Lots of small talk.
- √ Meeting is constantly interrupted by phone calls and others getting Al-Ajeib's attention.

In the Early Evening...

- √ Little Progress made.
- √ Time for dinner.
- √ Splendid meal at an exquisite restaurant.
- √ Al-Ajeib casually mentions that he would be able to agree with "the deal you want," for a modest commission.
- √ He also asks whether you like the dancers in the restaurant, hinting that "something could be arranged."

What's Going on Here?

- √ Different habits and practices.
- √ Different values.
- √ Different expectations.
- √ Different interpretations or behaviors.
- √ Different ethical views.

U.S. "Unwritten Negotiation Rules" - Lothar, Katz, 2014.

- √ Share at least all essential information.
- √ Don't lie.
- √ Don't get emotional.
- √ Make only reasonable offers.
- √ Don't take back what you previously committed.

√ Make a final offer only when it is really final.
√ Don't play for time unless you absolutely need to.
√ It is your responsibility to check the fine print.
√ A deal is a deal.

Environmental Factors Affecting International Negotiations.

Economic, Geographic, Security, Cultural, Legal/Political, Infrastructure and Ethical Conflicts in International Business

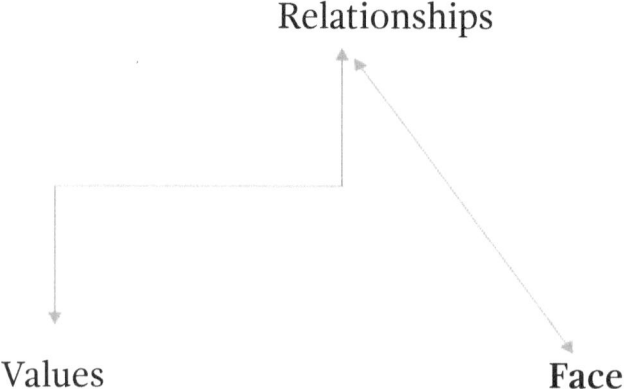

Values　　　　　　　　　　　　　Face

Ethics in International Negotiations

- Usually no agreement on "right or wrong" across different cultures.
- Legalistic arguments rarely help.
- Important to separate practices from intentions.
- Remain firm where you want to.
- Walk away when you have to. Otherwise, do what it takes to keep the relationship intact.
- Refrain from moralizing or criticizing a foreign counterpart for "unethical" conduct.
- Don't take anything personally.

Phases of Negotiations: How Time is Spent

1. Preparation
   - Relationship building.
2. Information gathering
   - Bargaining & Decision-Making
3. Agreement & Closure.

Nanjing Negotiations – China

- Nuvocor, and up-and-comer in the biopharmaceutical market, are looking for a supplier for custom vitals in China.
- They find a company in Nanjing, China, that seems well qualified and has sufficient production capacity to support substantial business growth.
- After initial negotiations via email, Nuvocor's Chief Procurement Officer briefly visits Nanjing on a trip across Asia and manages to work out a deal.

Nanjing Nuisance

- Initial deliveries look great.
- Several months later, a truck accident causes Nuvocor to lose a large batch of vials.
- Nuvocor sends an urgent request to the supplier in China, explaining the situation and asking for a special out-of-term delivery within a week.
- In spite of several more emails and voicemails, they don't even get a response from China until nine days after the request was made.

Task vs. Relationship Orientation

Task-Oriented (U.S., Germany & France	Relationship-Oriented 9India, China, Mexico & United Arab Emirates)
1. Getting the job done matters most.	1. Relationships matter most.
2. Will do business with an unknown person if it "makes sense."	2. May not do business with an unknown person.
3. Decision-making should be "blind," without favoritism to those affected.	3. Decision making requires involving all who may be affected.

Task vs. Relationship Oriented Countries

- Task-Oriented Countries:
√ Australia, Austria, Belgium, Canada, Denmark, Finland, France, Germany, Israel, Netherlands, New Zealand, Norway, Sweden, Switzerland, United Kingdom, United States.
- Some Relationship-Oriented Countries:
√ Afghanistan, Algeria, Bolivia, Brazil, Chile, China, Czech Republic (most Eastern European Countries), Cuba, Egypt, Haiti, Hungary, Iceland, Iraq, Iran, Jamaica, South Korea, Kuwait, Malaysia, Pakistan, India, Poland, Portugal, Russia, Saudi Arabia, Singapore, South Africa, Spain, Taiwan, Turkey, Ukraine, United Arab Emirates, Venezuela, Yemen, Zimbabwe.

American Negotiators Are Often...

1. Highly task-oriented
2. Impatient (time is money)

3. Averse to the thought of returning empty-handed.
4. Willing to make concessions in order to move things forward.
5. Less interested in a deal if it takes "too long."

Communication – Cultural Challenges

Group-Oriented Cultures vs. Individualistic

> √ (Task-oriented countries such as U.S. are Individualistic.
> √ Relationship-oriented countries such as China are Group-Oriented.
> - Group-oriented members are usually strongly interdependent.
> - "Us-versus-them" thinking is common.
> - Individuals may not want to stand out from the group.
> - Decisions are normally made by the group and primarily influenced by group interests rather than individual interests.

Challenges When Dealing with Members of Group-Oriented Culture

- The Concept of "Face"
  ▶ Being turned down or publicly criticized, failing to show respect, contradicting someone, losing one's temper, can all cause loss of face.
  ▶ Organizations have "Face" too. Improper behavior can make business connections difficult throughout a company.
  ▶ Giving a face is done by praising group or organizations, showing great respect, etc. Very important for relationship building.

Challenges When Dealing with Members of Group-Oriented Cultures

- **Indirect Communication:**
  ▶ People think it very important to "save face."
  ▶ Usually prefer giving evasive responses over saying "no"
  ▶ "Yes" may only mean "I hear you"
  ▶ The message that is being conveyed is often found between the lines, not directly in the words.

Examples:

- "Our management has requested further study"

- "Our limited budget may be a challenge"

- "We admire the creativity of your plan"

  ▶ Body language may convey a significant part of the "real" message.

Directness Example

The American, "I am not sure I agree"

The German, "That's not correct"

The Chinese, "You are a person of strong principles and the insight you provide is respected by many"

Check This Conversation in China Out!

▶ Mr. Narayanan, I am afraid we'll have to keep working on Saturday if we want to make our deadline.
▶ Mr. Diller, I see.
▶ Can you come in on Saturday to supervise the work?

- I think so
- I certainly appreciate it.
- Yes. Did you know that Saturday is a very special day?
- I am sorry
- My son will be turning 1o years old
- How nice. I hope you and your family enjoy it very much.
- Thank you for understanding.

Modeled after Craig Storti's Cross-Cultural Dialogues.

Secrets of Face-Saving Communication

- Emphasize positive aspects. Try to see issues from a 'glass half full' perspective and avoid talking about 'problems' or 'issues.' "We can deliver it in three days" is better than "We cannot do it in two days."
- Use vague language rather than saying "no." Try not to shut any doors.
- Make the issue one that both sides own. "we will need to solve this together" is better than "Our problem is this."
- Convey critical points through omission rather than by openly pointing them out. "Most of the code is complete" is better than "The user interface still has problems."

Five Deal-making Tips for Closing the Deal

Deal-making Tip #1. Diagnose the Barrier: When you've made progress on certain issues in deal-making but remain stymied on others in a negotiation, it's time to take a hard look at what's standing between you and a mutually acceptable deal.

Deal-making Tip #2. Use the Clock

Negotiations expand to fill the time available. We may not like to make important decisions under the gun, but deadlines can provide a healthy incentive for closing the deal. It's no accident that lawsuits settle on the courthouse steps and that strikes often are averted at the eleventh hour. Until that point, the daily costs of protracted negotiation may not seem high (though, clearly, they mount over time).

Only when the judge is about to be seated or the contract is due to expire are people jolted out of the relative comfort of the status quo. If you anticipate these moments, recognize your priorities, and keep channels of communication open, you'll be able to move quickly and wisely when you have to.

To avoid getting bogged down in never-ending talks, it pays to impose a deadline at the outset of negotiation. You also can put a fuse on the proposals you make, though exploding offers can backfire if the other party resents being put under artificial pressure.

Deal-making Tip #3. Count Your Change

Even if you've done everything right, you have to be alert for gambits and tricks as the negotiation winds down.

A classic bargaining tactic among lawyers advises, "After the agreement has been reached, have your client reject it and raise his demands." It's a common gambit for car salespeople, too, as they return from conferring with the manager. The news is never good: "You've got to offer $1,000 more – but he'll toss in the floor mats for free."

Shame on those who resort to such tired old ploys. Shame on you, too, if you're not ready for them.

When you're closing the deal, confirm that all the key provisions have been covered so there will be no surprises. Even after you've gotten a sincere handshake, your counterpart may come back with further demands if she is having a tough time selling the deal internally. (You'll sometimes be in that position yourself.)

From the outside, of course, it's impossible to know when you're being taken for a ride and when the need for revisions is legitimate. How the negotiation has gone up until that point may offer an important clue.

Either way, however, you should be leery about making any unreciprocated concessions. If your counterpart asks for new terms, even if you can afford them, you should get a favorable adjustment in return. Otherwise, you're simply encouraging further requests.

Ethical Views on International Negotiations.

Please read more on Ethical Views at the links below:

1. Program on Negotiations, Harvard Law School. Overcoming Cross-cultural Barriers to a Negotiated Agreement: Negotiation Ethics and International Negotiations. Click HERE https://www.pon.harvard.edu/daily/international-negotiation-daily/cultural-caveats-in-international-negotiations/
2. Ethics and Negotiations. PDF. World Academy of Science, Engineering and Technology Vol:5, No:6, 2011 Click HERE https://waset.org/publications/1279/ethics-in-negotiations-the-confrontation-between-representation-and-practices
3. Forbes. In Ethics Negotiations, Interest Matters. Click HERE https://www.forbes.com/sites/jimcamp/2013/10/22/in-ethics-negotiations-interests-matter/#3b6a83ac7036

Exercise.

1. State and explain three (3) main ideas of how you will negotiate to partner with a retail business in Saudi Arabia to get more customers there. Will your negotiation style

change if you are negotiating with the same organization in Egypt? Why or why not?
2. For this assessment, you will **write a 3-page reflective** paper on this:

Your organization, Brains Consults, sent you to China to negotiate on partnering with Chengen Consult, a Chinese consulting firm so that you can work together in the Chinese business market.

Explain by giving a step-by-step account of how you will negotiate with them to strike a deal and how you plan on dealing with:

1. Different consulting practices.
2. Different values.
3. Different expectations.
4. Different interpretations (give examples) or behaviors.
5. Different ethical views.

Please make sure to have a cover page, introduction, respond to the prompt (from a-e), good analysis using negotiating words and techniques learned this week, conclusions and references if you cited other works. Avoid errors by using spelling checks. The paper must not be less than three pages, excluding the cover page.

Writing Grant: For Non-profits

GRANT WRITING IS a business practice of completing an application process for a financial grant or assistance provided by an institution such as a government department, corporation, foundation or trust. Both for-profit and non-profit organizations write grants. Educational institutions also write grants to seek funding for important research. The first step in grant writing is to find the right grant for you. The second step is to sit down and write that winning proposal.

So, what should be included in your grant application? Your grant proposals should be split into four categories:

- Needs
- Approach
- Outcomes and
- Future funding.

Needs

- Describe the need addressed by your project (issues, events, threat assessments or vulnerabilities).
- Include an independent justification for addressing the problem. Consider additional local, regional and state requirements driving the project.

- Link to contextual drivers that support your desire to conduct the project now.

Approach

- Describe the project concisely. Document the nature and scope of the project. Include any details that help explain your specific plans for the funding.
- Highlight advantages to this project over alternative solutions. Discuss other approaches you have considered locally and why you chose the solution you did.

Outcomes

- List anticipated benefits. Be sure to relate the outcomes to your initial discussion of needs. The more localized the better.
- Include a chart detailing expected outcomes, suggested indicators, targets and time-frames. When possible, replace general outcomes with specific metrics you will report to the funder at the end of the funding period.

Future Funding

- Describe your plan to ensure continued maintenance of the program.
- Include specific plans to fund future roll-out of additional modules, if needed.

Grant Tip: Always start with the grant guidance or program website to see if the funder has provided a specific application form or list of questions. If so, be sure to follow those directions fully and completely.

A Good Example of Grant Writing for the Police by a Sheriff.

One of the best ways to learn how to write a grant proposal is to look at other successful grants from other law enforcement agencies.

This question was asked on a 2015 Body-Worn Camera Pilot Program:

Application Question: Demonstrate a full understanding of how officer complaints and use of force practices can be addressed by the police in Pittsburgh.

A great, winning answer was this:

The City continues struggling with growing civilian-police tensions. In 2014, 280 misconduct complaints were filed against Pittsburgh police officers. Allegations such as these fall into four categories: conduct unbecoming a member, conduct towards the public, warrantless searches and seizures, and use of force. Below, these numbers are broken down along with an estimate of whether a relatively new tool for police, Body-Worn Cameras (BWCs), would have been relevant to the investigation of these allegations, based on the presence of conflicting narratives between the officer and complainant in each case:

Pittsburgh Police Misconduct Complaints Category

Pittsburgh Police Misconduct Complaints by Category, 2014			
	Total Complaints (#)	BWCs would have aided in investigation* (#)	BWCs would have aided in investigation* (%)
Conduct Unbecoming a Member	80	32	40%
Conduct Towards the Public	128	118	92%
Warrantless Searches and Seizures	26	23	88%
Use of Force	46	41	89%
TOTAL	**280**	**214**	**76%**

BWC recordings, also referred to as Digital Multimedia Evidence (DME), serve as the best, most objective evidence of what actually happened during a reported incident. This can have substantial impact: the existence of BWC recordings will protect officers against fabricated accusations by civilians and perhaps most importantly for the City of Pittsburgh, incidents involving the use-of-force need no longer be the subject of competing stories. DME recordings will show whether use-of-force was warranted and proper procedures used. DME can also highlight instances when training or departmental policy would benefit from an overall change. For additional resource, read Forbes. Nine traits of effective grant writers.

Tips if You're Not A Grant Writer

Prepare to dive in:

- The end result, those neatly typed pages you'll one day hand over, will exist only because of the time and energy you invest in crafting an insightful and thoroughly researched proposal.
- Your proposal will be a mix of facts, figures and stories that show the impact of your what you do and the kind of help/fund you need along with detailed accounts of your project's timeline and objectives.
- Begin by creating an outline of the entire proposal. Getting a few things organized before you start putting your thoughts on paper will go a long way to support your process.
- **Get buy-in from coworkers.** Talk with everyone who will be involved in the outcome before you begin working on content. Plan a meeting with as many stakeholders as you can gather. Even a 30-minute brainstorming session can better inform the content of your proposal. Come prepared with questions, such as: How will we measure success? Who will be responsible for organizing reports

to the funder? What is the ideal timeline for use of these funds should we be awarded the grant?
- **Make sure that your work matches the interests and aims of the funders.** Sometimes, in a rush to get a bunch of proposals out the door, organizations apply for grants that don't truly align with their work and mission. Trying to bend your program to fit a foundation's guidelines can make things harder for you in the long run. Skip these applications and keep looking. Your time can be better spent elsewhere!
- **Go over the foundation's requirements carefully.** You want to know exactly what information the foundation wants from you as you'll likely be the one to collect and collate that information from program staff. Help them out by giving them plenty of time and a structure within which to collect and organize their part of the work. Let people know exactly what you need and when you need it—preferably a couple of months ahead of time! Send along friendly reminders to check in and offer support.

Exercise:

Write a Grant Request to Access Funding for a hypothetical Non-profit Children Organization

- Make sure to check their grant Guidelines and Grant Request Application at their website.
- The grant request should not be more than three (3) pages.

Take AIM in Conflict Resolution

EVERY MANAGER STRUGGLES with how to deal with conflict as an intervention strategy. However, the ability to effectively resolve conflict can be the difference between success and failure, job satisfaction or dissatisfaction, and a productive team or an apathetic one. It is estimated that 50% of managers' time is spent in dealing with conflicts (Penguin Publishing Group). Fifty Percent! The cost of that time –not even considering lost sales and productivity – is enormous. These are the consequences of conflict at the workplace: projects are derailed, unresolved conflicts steal energy from the manager and the team, negative impact on productivity; missed targets, goals and deadline. That is why resolving conflict is the most important decision at the workplace.

What do you think of when you hear that word...Conflict!

- ▶ Many people say things like:
- ▶ It makes me anxious and stressed out
- ▶ I feel frustrated when conflicts come up on my team because I know they will eat up time I'd planned for other work.
- ▶ I lose my head and say things I later wish I hadn't.
- ▶ I feel bad for my family because sometimes I take the stress from a work conflict home with me.
- ▶ Conflict is a huge pain in the neck

Thus, dealing with conflict is the hardest thing about the job of a manager.

NOTE

- ▶ Conflict is NOT inherently negative as you think. It is our interpretation of and response to conflict that is the most negative.
- ▶ Conflict is inevitable – it is a normal aspect of human interaction.
- ▶ Conflict arises from unmet needs, unrecognized differences, and difficulties in coping with life changes and challenges – things that occur in offices and homes everywhere, every day.
- ▶ Conflict is simply a part of life

Good News!

- ▶ Conflict can lead to progress if handled calmly, skillfully and appropriately.
- ▶ Conflict is an opportunity to create positive change.
- ▶ Think about it. Most of the inventions, discoveries and technological advances made throughout history have been the results of humans developing solutions to conflicts, whether they were conflicts with other people, other nations, nature, our immediate surroundings, even the cells that make up our bodies.
- ▶ It is the disagreements among scientists, explorers and philosophers that lead us to learn and understand more about our world and ourselves.
- ▶ Therefore, high performing managers understand that opportunity is often disguised as conflict.

Resolving Conflict – Possible Responses

"For every minute you remain angry, you give up sixty seconds of peace of mind." – Ralph Waldo Emerson.

We tend to deal with Conflict in Three Ways:

a. Ignore it: Natural response is to ignore it and hope it goes away. But when a conflict is ignored, it doesn't go away, it rather escalates.
b. Respond emotionally or irrationally: This happens because we tend to take comments, situations and events personally.
c. Resolve it effectively: Deal with the conflict and resolve it quickly, effectively and with less stress for all those involved. This is the best approach.

Resolving Conflicts – Take AIM

▶ **In resolving conflict, use the AIM acronym.**

❋ Attitude – Your positive beliefs and thoughts about the conflict

❋ Intention – the outcome or result you'd like to achieve

❋ Message – how you communicate your intention, both verbally and nonverbally.

Why use the AIM Technique?

▶ Resolves the conflict and enhances the relationship
▶ Facilitates the best possible results for the organization
▶ Ensures high performance and improves productivity
▶ Leads to a better work environment and experience.

√ There is a caveat for using AIM: The approach requires that you care or are willing to start caring about the dignity of all the people involved in the conflict.

Resolving Conflict Takes EFFORT

▶ Explain your intention. Add any information that may help both parties.

▶ Find a common ground. Identify many possible areas of consensus.

▶ Flexibility is crucial. Commit to maintaining an open mind.

▶ Options. Brainstorm potential solutions to satisfy all parties.

▶ Resolve the conflict. First ask the other party(ies): "Do you think I've listened to your concerns with an open mind? Have we considered everyone's viewpoint and all the important information?

▶ Take action. End the discussion with a precise understanding and agreement; and specific action that will follow. Give specific time frame.

What NOT To Do

▶ Avoid the conflict at all cost - maybe the problem will just go away.
▶ React on the spot without thinking.
▶ Take things personally.
▶ If someone is highly emotional, tell the person to "calm down"
▶ When attacked, attack back.
▶ Handle the conflict via email.
▶ Say the "right" words without being sincere.

- ▶ Push the discussion no matter how upset you or the other person gets.
- ▶ Focus only on your interests and forget the interests of others.
- ▶ Jump into conflict resolution discussions without adjusting your Attitude and writing your Intention.

What to do when you can't resolve conflict Face-to-Face?

- ▶ Many managers lead people who are not in the same office building, town or even country. Distance certainly doesn't eliminate conflicts. Remember Never to resolve any conflict via email.
- ▶ Pick up the phone and have a conversation, live and in real time!
- ▶ While on the phone...
- √ Pay extra attention to your tone of voice to be sure you sound as you intend.
- √ Eliminate distractions that could take your focus away from the conversation.
- √ Paraphrase the other person intermittently to be sure her intention and your intention are being heard correctly.
- √ Listen for the other person's nonverbal messages that are inconsistent with what is spoken, such as hesitations, uncertain tone, etc.
- √ Please be real!

What to do when confronted with a highly emotional response

- ▶ Acknowledge the other person's emotions before offering your message.
- ▶ Look beyond the situation at hand, search for the bigger issue and take your best guess as to what is really going on.
- ▶ If you've correctly identified the bigger issue, find common ground by sincerely letting the person know that you agree with his/her concern.

Remember to always address the emotion and/or its cause first. Sometimes a statement recognizing the situation is all you need to reduce the emotional intensity.

What to do when caught in a surprise attack.

- ▶ "Remember not only to say the right thing in the right place, but far more difficult still, to leave unsaid the wrong thing at the tempting moment." Benjamin Franklin.
- When caught in a surprise attack,
- √ Ask for a time-out. Take time out to regroup and approach the conflict in a constructive manner.
- √ Use the "best friend" technique. This is a mindset strategy of thinking of a person in your life whom you trust completely to stand for your best interests, perhaps your best friend.
- √ Remember when it comes to surprise attack, it is NOT about jumping in; it is about stepping back.

What to do when you sense the potential for violence.

"You can't shake hands with a clenched fist." Indira Gandhi.

- If you sense violence, stop the discussion and get to safety.
- When it comes to violent conflicts, it is NOT about resolution, it is about safety.

Preventive Maintenance.

"The people to fear are not those who disagree with you, but those who disagree with you and are too cowardly to let you know." – Joe Moore.

Preventive maintenance techniques can keep small disagreements from becoming larger conflicts. This is when an ounce of prevention can be worth several pounds of your favorite headache remedy.

- √ Use AIM and EFFORT strategies. Your "Intent" is crucial.
- √ Take note and take action when someone's nonverbal behaviors don't match what they say.
- √ It is not about what people say; it is about what they want to say.

10 Ways To Keep Conflicts from Escalating.

1. Get all the facts and clearly identify the problem.
2. Encourage people to challenge the status quo early so that all different opinions are on the table from the outset.
3. Do your best to see the positive in situations and people.
4. Be willing to listen and consider all viewpoints, especially those you disagree with.
5. When others explain their intention and viewpoints, summarize and paraphrase to confirm understanding.
6. Look for common ground in any difficult situation.
7. When possible, resolve one issue at a time.
8. Deal with the molehills before they become mountains.
9. Only send and respond to e-mails that are informational in nature. If there is any hint of disagreement, meet in person or pick up a phone.
10. Watch and listen for inconsistencies between people's words and their nonverbal behaviors and encourage them to voice their concerns.

Sharpening Your AIM

"The skill to do comes from the doing." – Cicero.

- ▶ You will be great in managing and resolving conflicts at the workplace by doing. Keep addressing conflicts using techniques in these notes.
- ▶ Teach your team how to effectively resolve conflicts for themselves with the AIM approach. Then be a coach and cheerleader.

Conflict Resolution Summary: Take AIM at the Conflict:

Attitude – Is my attitude toward the situation and the people involved positive?

Intention – Is my intention to find the best possible outcome for all concerned and enhance the relationship? My intention is (Write your intention below):

Message: AM I prepared to express my intention sincerely, both verbally and nonverbally?

Conflict Resolution Summary – Give the discussion your best EFFORT

- ▶ **E**xplain – Sincerely share my intention and encourage others to share theirs.
- ▶ **F**ind – Find a common ground, as many areas of agreement as possible.
- ▶ **F**lexibility – Keep an open mind and be ready to consider any number of possibilities, including a solution that's not mine.
- ▶ **O**ptions – Brainstorm potential solutions to resolve the conflict in a way that will satisfy all parties.
- ▶ **R**esolve - Decide on a solution that addresses common interests and that everyone can support.
- ▶ **T**ake Action – Leave the discussion with a clear understanding of future actions, including the "who, what and when."

Exercise.

You are a manager and Tonya is a member of your team, and two of you are having a disagreement about her performance review. Tonya believes she should receive an "exceeds expectations," while you believe her performance only met expectations. How will you use the AIM and EFFORT techniques to resolve the conflict? This analysis must be five pages.

Business Case for Diversity and Inclusion (D&I).

WE BEGIN THIS chapter with this question: Why is diversity and inclusion important? Because it is not about the job that keeps people at the workplace, but the community as well. D&I is about understanding different perspectives and benefits to your organization. **First, it is a great thing to admit that we are all different in one way or the other.** That is the beauty of our universe! **Second, it is important to admit that we all have biases, conscious or unconscious emanating from where you grew up.** Business managers need data to drive their D&I planned priorities. The diversity part of color, age, sex, etc. is easy to measure. We grew up surrounded by different colors, heights, disabilities, etc. what does that familiarity do to you? If you pay attention to D&I, what will be the outcome for your business? The tangible takes away is, what can you do as a business to enhance D&I? **The difficult one to measure is the Inclusion piece. Most Asian countries are moving from D&I to cultural celebrations because of the difficulty of "Who is including who"** in the D&I process.

In a cultural studies, Langer and Austin identified the following as main factors of our "cultural eye:"

a. Spiritual Beliefs
b. Education
c. Race
d. Age
e. Gender
f. Social Class, and
g. Political beliefs

Guidelines for Culturally Competent Leadership Celebrating Cultural Differences & Diversity

Top 6 areas to cause the greatest challenges in diversity and varied groups:

1. Time and Space
2. Fate and Personal Responsibility
3. Face-Saving & Disclosure
4. Communication – Verbal & Non-Verbal
5. Conflict Avoidance or Conflict Use
6. Decision making and ways of knowing

In a world as complex as ours, each of us is shaped by many factors, and culture is one of the powerful forces that acts on us. Anthropologists Kevin Avruch and Peter Black explain the importance of culture this way:

...One's own culture provides the "lens" through which we view the world; the "logic"... by which we order it; the "grammar" ... by which it makes sense. In other words, culture is central to what we see, how we make sense of what we see, and how we express ourselves.

As people from different, diverse cultural groups take on the exciting challenge of working together, cultural values sometimes conflict. We can misunderstand each other, and react in ways that can hinder what are otherwise promising partnerships. Oftentimes, we aren't aware that culture is acting upon us. Sometimes, we are not even aware that we have cultural values or assumptions that are different from others. As you set to work on multicultural collaboration in your leadership and life, keep in mind these additional guidelines:

- Know that you don't know everything and **be willing to learn, ask questions and show genuine interest**.
- Learn from generalizations about other cultures, but **don't use those generalizations to stereotype**, judge, "write off," or oversimplify your ideas about another person.
- **Practice**, practice, practice. That's the first rule, because it's in the doing that we actually get better at cross-cultural communication.
- Don't assume that there is one right way (yours!) to communicate. **Keep questioning your assumptions** about the "right way" to communicate. For example, think about your body language; postures that indicate receptivity in one culture might indicate aggressiveness in another.
- Don't assume that breakdowns in communication occur because other people are on the wrong track. **Search for ways to make the communication work**, rather than searching for who should receive the blame for the breakdown.
- **Listen actively and empathetically**. Try to put yourself in the other person's shoes. Especially when another person's perceptions or ideas are very different from your own, you might need to operate at the edge of your own comfort zone.
- **Respect others' choices** about whether to engage in communication with you. Honor their opinions about what is going on.

- Stop, suspend judgment, and try **to look at the situation as an outsider and their perspective.**
- **Be prepared for a discussion of the past.** Use this as an opportunity to develop an understanding from "the other's" point of view, rather than getting defensive or impatient. Acknowledge historical events that have taken place. Be open to learning more about them. **Honest acknowledgment of the mistreatment and oppression** that have taken place on the basis of cultural difference is vital for effective communication.
- **Awareness of current power imbalances** -- and an openness to hearing each other's perceptions of those imbalances -- is also necessary for understanding each other and working together.
- Remember that **cultural norms may not apply to the behavior of any particular individual**. We are all shaped by many, many factors -- our ethnic background, our family, our education, our personalities -- and are more complicated than any cultural norm could suggest. Check your interpretations if you are uncertain what is meant.

Learning about people's cultures has the potential to give us a mirror image of our own. We have the opportunity to challenge our assumptions about the "right" way of doing things, and consider a variety of approaches. We have a chance to learn new ways to solve problems that we had previously given up on, accepting the difficulties as "just the way things are."

Lastly, if we are open to learning about people from other cultures, we become less lonely. Prejudice and stereotypes separate us from whole groups of people who could be friends and partners in working for change. Many of us long for real contact. Talking with people different from ourselves gives us hope and energizes us to take on the challenge of improving our communities and worlds.

Respecting Our Differences and Working Together

In addition to helping us to understand ourselves and our own cultural frames of reference, knowledge of these six patterns of cultural difference can help us to understand the people who are different from us. An appreciation of patterns of cultural difference can assist us in processing what it means to be different in ways that are respectful of others, not faultfinding or damaging.

Anthropologists Avruch and Black have noted that, when faced by an interaction that we do not understand, people tend to interpret the others involved as "abnormal," "weird," or "wrong." This tendency, if indulged, gives rise on the individual level to prejudice. If this propensity is either consciously or unconsciously integrated into organizational structures, then prejudice takes root in our institutions; in the structures, laws, policies, and procedures that shape our lives. Consequently, **it is vital that we learn to control the human tendency to translate "different from me" into "less than me."** We can learn to do this.

We can also learn to collaborate across cultural lines as individuals and as a society. Awareness of cultural differences doesn't have to divide us from each other. It doesn't have to paralyze us either, for fear of not saying the "right thing." In fact, becoming more aware of our cultural differences, as well as exploring our similarities, can help us communicate with each other more effectively. Recognizing where cultural differences are at work is the first step toward understanding and respecting each other.

Learning about different ways that people communicate can enrich our lives. People's different communication styles reflect deeper philosophies and world views which are the foundation of their culture. Understanding these deeper philosophies gives us a broader picture of what the world has to offer us.

Cultural Competency Journey Model Exercise

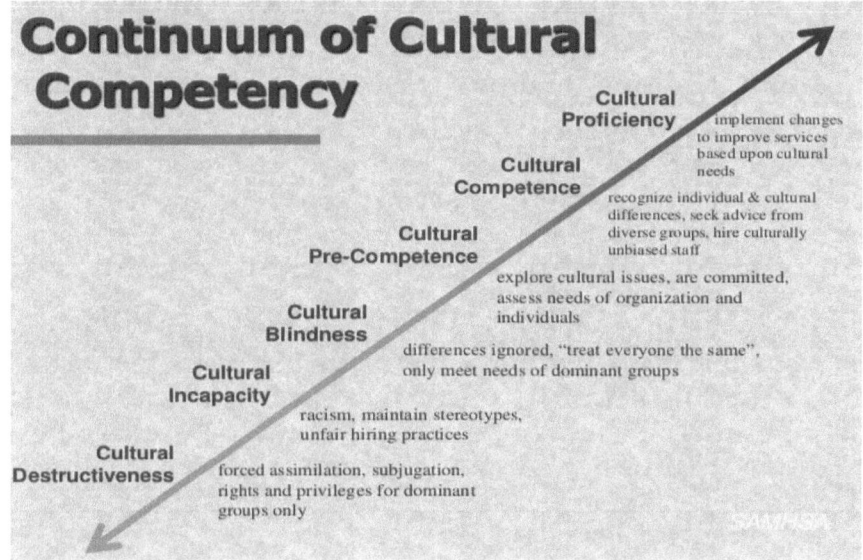

Introduction: We are all at different places in our 'cultural competency journey' where we learn more ourselves and others. Maybe you have been exploring these topics for a long time or maybe you are brand new to this and are just starting out. So, this is a chance for you to assess where you are and to find what you need.

Instructions:

1. **Complete the Self-Assessment Table** on the next page by putting an X in the column that you think best represents you at this time and review your answers.
2. **Using your answers, Go to the link below** and explore what it provides. There is an enormous amount of information, links to other sites and useful tools.
3. After exploring the LINK, **Identify 2 STEPS** that you are going to go deeper on. Then, explore each of the topics/areas in that step in greater depth (see examples below).

4. After exploring and completing the activities, **Describe what you found** and **Summarize what you learned**. I have copied the website onto the next page to assist with recall after you have finished exploring and are doing your write-up.
5. Then, provide at least 3 ways that you think you can expand your cultural competency in the page below.

PROFESSIONAL Cultural Competency Self- Assessment				
READ EACH STATEMENT BELOW AND THEN PLACE AN 'X' IN THE BOX THAT BEST MATCHES YOU.	Yes, I DO	I have not but I PLAN to SOON	I hope to but I don't know HOW	I have NO interest in doing this
I seek out more information to enhance my own awareness and understanding of racism by talking with others, reading or listening.				
I have spent time recently looking at my own attitudes and behaviors as they contribute to or combat racism, sexism, able-ism and other forms of prejudice around me.				
I have re-evaluated my use of terms or phrases that may be perceived by others as degrading or hurtful.				
I have suggested, initiated, or attended workshops or discussions with friends, colleagues, social clubs or church groups about cultural diversity and inclusion.				

I have openly disagreed with a racist, sexist, homophobic or able-ist comment, action or joke.				
I have made a personal contract with myself to take a positive stand on cultural diversity and inclusion.				
When I see a broadcast, advertisement or read a newspaper article that is racially, sexually, ability, culturally or religiously biased, I have complained to the person in charge.				
I have talked with my colleagues at work about the racial/cultural/diversity climate in our college.				
I have examined my course's curricula, textbooks, materials and other items for race, gender, ability, age, religion and cultural balance.				
I have made a commitment to learn more about a culture that is different from my own, through reading, study and listening.				
I have supported, contributed time and /or funds to an agency, fund or program that promotes diversity and inclusion.				
Identify another personal activity / action you have taken to promote diversity and inclusion BELOW:				

LINK: Please go to http://www.lacrosseconsortium.org/content/c/personal_journey **to explore this site.**

EXAMPLE: For example, say I am curious about Step 2: Am You Truly Self-Aware? I will open all of the links and materials for that topic, read and explore them and then provide a brief description of what I explored and a summary of what I learned. For my second step, I may want to do step #5 'The Other Side of Privilege' so I would explore all of the links, activities and resources in that step as well. Then I would describe what I found and what I learned.

You may agree or disagree with the material – that is fine. Describe what you found and then provide your reasoning as to why you agree/disagree with it. Then find another step to explore and write-up. You are encouraged to explore ALL of the steps but you only need to write-up 2 steps below.

4. Write a summary of what you found:

STEP # ? _____ (←select the 1st step you want to explore and it's title →) **Step Title:**

Description of what I found:

Summary of what I learned:

STEP # ? _____ (←select the 2nd step you want to explore and it's title →) **Step Title:**

Description of what I found:

Summary of what I learned:

3 ways I can expand my cultural competency:

1.

2.

3.

21 Ways to Stop a Conversation about Diversity

Instruction: Circle the ones you've said before and put an "X" by the ones you can't understand why they would stop a conversation on diversity.

1. I don't see color. We're all just human beings.

2. We have more similarities than differences.

3. I think deep down we're all the same.

4. Racism/sexism happens all over the world.

5. I think some people use diversity as an excuse.

6. I think identifying into groups only further divides us.

7. There are lots of other diversity issues other than race and gender.

8. I've never seen that happen before. Are you sure it happened?

9. Why does everything have to be so politically correct?

10. I was just joking.

11. Things are a lot better than they used to be. Don't you agree?

12. We'd hire more women and people of color, but are they qualified?

13. I love everyone.

14. Do you really think it's that bad?

15. I'm so glad you're not like one of them.

16. You know, you're a credit to your people.

17. You don't see other races complaining.

18. I think its reverse racism/sexism.

19. America is the best place to live.

20. Some of my best friends are colored.

21. You speak such good English, where did you learn it from?

Excerpted from The Art of Mindful Facilitation by Lee Mun Wah. Copyright © 2004.

Unconscious Bias.

Foster an Inclusive Culture by Taking the Time to Recognize Your Unconscious Biases. Knowing your bias is important even if you are not in a position of hiring or firing. Fostering an inclusive and diverse culture in your organization is about much more than hiring practices. People can take steps to support diversity and inclusion every day in their interactions with colleagues. One of the best ways to do that is to become more aware of your unconscious biases and take steps to mitigate them. No one is immune from having biases, and often they do not arise from any ill intent. The Nobel-prize winning economist Daniel Kahneman, most widely known as the author of the best-selling book "Thinking, Fast and Slow," did seminal work identifying many of these biases and the reasons we form them. As Dr. Kahneman explains, our brain really has two operating systems. System one enables us to do things, like drive our cars, almost on automatic pilot, without much conscious thinking required. System two works when we must be fully present and alert, making every decision about what to do or say next.

The problem is that System one, our unconscious brain, often operates with assumptions that prove to be false. This stems from the fact that our brain must quickly organize and classify the millions of impressions we are hit with every day. But the leaps we take may not hold up under more careful consideration. Some of the errors in perception that our unconscious brain can make include:

Similar-to-me bias: When we put greater stock in the thoughts and opinions of people who feel familiar to us because they're of the same cultural background or same gender or have a similar personality.

Confirmation bias: When we attach greater significance to evidence that proves one of our existing opinions.

Recency bias: When we allow ourselves to be overly influenced by our most recent experience.

Systemic bias: When we don't pay enough attention to an embedded system or process that immediately puts certain groups of people at a disadvantage.

Strategies for Keeping an Open Mind.

Even when the impact of our biases is brought to our attention, it can be easy to insist we aren't falling prey to them. Orchestra leaders, for example, may believe they are simply hiring the best musicians, without any gender bias. But what happens if their decisions are put to the test? In a famous case from the early 1950s, the Boston Symphony Orchestra decided to have auditioning musicians play behind a curtain and also enter the stage on a carpet. (In a first round of the test, the gender bias had crept in, even with the curtain, because the judges could tell the difference in the sounds heels vs. men's flat-soled shoes made on a stage's wooden floors.) When the tests were fully blind, 50% of the women candidates advanced to the next stage of the auditions – a far higher rate of women than had ever been passed through before. These findings have clear implications for hiring managers.

When Interviewing: When interviewing candidates for your organization, start by identifying the professional qualifications of the ideal candidate. Take a look at your broader team and give some thought to what skill sets are missing, who you currently have on the team, and what kind of candidate would be able to provide diverse perspectives and complement your existing team. A second bias-mitigation strategy is to consider who should be part of the interview process, taking time to ensure that the interviewers bring a mixture of perspective and experience. A third strategy is to make a list, before reviewing someone's resume, of all the assumptions you would make based on things like the town they live in, the college they went to, and how long they stayed in past jobs. Simply by writing out your assumptions, you can begin to shift your brain from System one to System two. That shift can enable you to screen the candidate with a more objective and open mind. In a subsequent interview with the candidate, you will be more likely to uncover information and gain insights that demonstrate why the candidate would be a good fit. Overall, your hiring process will likely lead to better results when you make this effort to acknowledge and mitigate biases and involve multiple interviewers, who each bring their unique perspective.

At first impression, people often think diversity and inclusion is about creating a more accepting environment for people of different ethnic backgrounds, gender, and gender identity/sexual orientation. Inclusiveness is about much more than just accepting the differences.

It is about making sure that all employees feel welcome and are invited to be part of the dialogue, have access to opportunities for growth and development, and feel comfortable bringing their "whole self to work."

Evidently, most honest organizations open to diversity know these changes can be difficult to implement on their own and that is why they offer unconscious bias training to every employee. This training should do much more than enhance the organization's culture. It rather helps them perform better as a business. The research shows that diverse teams that are managed well tend to generate better results because of the diverse perspectives they bring and their ability to challenge each other's thinking. As a result, they also tend to develop more innovative solutions. One of the reasons for a diverse group's success may be that working alongside people who don't mirror us forces us out of our System one patterns of thinking and requires us to be more

Top Ten Diversity Best Practices

- Strong support from top management and board chair (written statement of commitment)
- Diversity linked to the strategic planning process, mission, vision
- "Diversity" or "Inclusion" identified as a core value for the organization in the appropriate documents (see also the first item on this list)
- Management reporting systems track, and allow leadership to set goals as appropriate, for "representation" for board membership, at the senior official's level, managers, and supervisors level, and across business units so that the organization's employees and volunteers (especially in leadership positions) 'look like the membership, (desired) customer base, or general population
- A diversity orientation is provided for new employees and follow-up sessions are offered for all staff, as appropriate, to address the organization's policies and procedures related to valuing and leveraging diversity to accomplish the organization's mission and achieve its vision (ALL employees are expected to attend and participate; leaders model this expectation by attending meetings).
- A diverse group of speakers at meetings.
- Meetings are accessible.
- Encourage speakers to address aspects of diversity in all presentations.
- Understanding the makeup of membership tracking various demographics of the membership, leadership, and staff to understand "representation."
- Mentoring, scholarship or other programs to encourage greater access and participation for under-represented segments of membership or society
- Diversity awareness training for the board, volunteers, and members

- Advertise employment opportunities to a diverse group of potential employees Scan all publications to ensure that offending images are removed, pictures include a culturally diverse group of people, and that language is neutral.
- Promote your trade or profession to minorities through career days at minority educational institutions or professional internships for minority students.
- Provide members with a list of resources for exploring cultural diversity issues.

Developed by ASAE's Diversity Committee (2016).

How to Overcome the Preference to Prejudice

Alistair Berg/Digital Vision/Getty Images

Prejudice can be defined as "pre-judging" and "any preconceived opinion or feeling, either favorable or unfavorable." Almost everyone has prejudices. However, at its worst, prejudice can lead to discrimination, confrontation and violence. Teaching us to avoid making prejudiced and biased opinions is important. Overcoming the tendency to prejudice is important for all of us and helps us build a better family, workplace, community, nation and world. Below are some of the best practices to avoid prejudices:

- **Get to know someone** before judging them. Spend some time talking to them before making judgments. Do not judge a person because of gender, ethnicity, or other physical characteristics.
- Learn about **cultures and countries** other than your own. Read books or watch programs about the beliefs and practices of other cultures.
- **Treat others the way you would like to be treated.** Before you do or say something mean to someone, ask yourself "How would I feel if someone said or did that to me?"

- **Defend someone who is being judged.** Do not join in if someone is making prejudiced remarks about another person.
- **Learn to tolerate differences in beliefs.** It is impossible for everyone to agree on everything. Find things, ideas, values and beliefs that you do have in common.
- Tackle the issue head on by encouraging schools, colleges, universities and employers **to talk about stereotypes and prejudice in their classrooms and businesses.** Discuss racism, anti-Semitism, sexism, homophobia, and other biases.
- **Investigate different stereotypes, where they came from, and how they impact people's views of one another.** Through such discussions, preteen and teenage students can gain a better understanding of the unfairness of prejudices and the dangers of stereotyping an entire group of people.
- **Promote education about different cultures.** Teach students about different races, ethnicities, religions and other groups to help students know the truth about people who are different from themselves. Becoming familiar with other cultures also removes the fear that can come from things that are different and may seem odd.

Changing people's attitudes and institutional practices is quite difficult but necessary work. A commitment among individuals, organizations, and institutions to valuing diversity is essential for healthy communities. Changes will not happen overnight, but you can begin to take small **Steps towards making a difference**. Small steps build the foundation for more organized, deeper, and larger efforts to build inclusive communities and makes everyone healthier, happier, more productive and more fulfilled.

Why is it important to reduce racial prejudice and racism?

Racism hurts EVERYONE!!

Racism is ILLEGAL!!

It goes against the democratic ideals upon which the United States was founded.

It is morally, ethically, and spiritually wrong and is against religious values.

It prevents people from reaching their full potential as human beings and assaults their humanness.

It prevents people from their full contribution to society and diminishes the people that practice racism.

Beliefs and systems of racism overlap with beliefs and systems of discrimination against many groups and include sexism, homophobia, ableism, ageism, classism, etc. By addressing and stopping racism, you will also be working against prejudice and discrimination against many others.

How can you reduce racial prejudice and racism?

AT WORK:

- As a worker, support and advocate for recruiting and hiring a racially and ethnically diverse staff.
- As a supervisor/manager, actively recruit and hire a racially and ethnically diverse staff.
- Talk to the people of color on your staff and ask them what barriers or attitudes they face at work.

- Examine company newsletter or other publications and look out for lack of visibility, negative portrayals, exclusion, or stereotypes.
- Work to actively promote inclusion and fight racism in your workplace.
- Speak out when you see or hear racism occurring. Everyone should be outraged at racism and stand up.

AT SCHOOL:

- Work to include anti-racism education in your school's curriculum. Work to change racist policies in your school.
- Promote Diversity. Try to support events that celebrate different cultural and ethnic groups.
- Organize vigils, anti-racism demonstrations, protests, or rallies if racism should occur.
- Examine school textbooks, newsletter or other publications and look for lack of visibility, negative portrayals, exclusion, or stereotypes.

IN YOUR LIFE:

- Make a commitment to speak up when you hear racial slurs, remarks or stereotypes that show racial prejudice.
- Make it a point to learn something new about different cultures.
- Think about ways to improve your workplace to promote racial understand and equity. Be proactive about making suggestions.
- Learn about other religions and races and give your child opportunities to attend events about other cultures.
- Help others who don't know about the history and oppression of different groups to better understand and share why you have taken a stand against racism.

10 THINGS EVERYONE SHOULD KNOW ABOUT RACE

Our eyes tell us that people look different. Most of us can tell the difference between black, brown, red and blonde hair. But what do those physical differences mean? Are they biological? Has race always been with us? How does race affect people today?

There's less - and more - to race than meets the eye – based on SCIENTIFIC EVIDENCE:

1. **Race is a modern idea.** Ancient societies, like the Greeks, did not divide people according to physical distinctions, but according to religion, status, class, even language. The English language didn't even have the word 'race' until it turns up in 1508 in a poem by William Dunbar referring to a line of kings.
2. **Race has no genetic basis.** Not one characteristic, trait or even gene distinguishes all the members of one so-called race from all the members of another so-called race.
3. **Human subspecies don't exist.** Unlike many animals, modern humans simply haven't been around long enough or isolated enough to evolve into separate subspecies or races. Despite surface appearances, we are one of the most similar of all species.
4. **Skin color really is only skin deep.** Most traits are inherited independently from one another. The genes influencing skin color have nothing to do with the genes influencing hair form, eye shape, blood type, musical talent, athletic ability or forms of intelligence. Knowing someone's skin color doesn't necessarily tell you anything else about him or her.
5. **Most variation is within, not between, "races."** Of the small amount of total human variation, 85% exists within any local population, be they Italians, Kurds, Koreans or Cherokees. About 94% can be found within any continent.

That means two random Koreans may be as genetically different as a Korean and an Italian.

6. **Slavery predates race.** Throughout much of human history, societies have enslaved others, often as a result of conquest or war, even debt, but not because of physical characteristics or a belief in natural inferiority. Due to a unique set of historical circumstances, ours was the first slave system where all the slaves shared similar physical characteristics.

7. **Race and freedom evolved together.** The U.S. was founded on the radical new principle that "All men are created equal." But our early economy was based largely on slavery. How could this anomaly be rationalized? The new idea of race helped explain why some people could be denied the rights and freedoms that others took for granted.

8. **Race justified social inequalities as natural.** As the race idea evolved, white superiority became "common sense" in America. It justified not only slavery but also the extermination of Indians, exclusion of Asian immigrants, and the taking of Mexican lands by a nation that professed a belief in democracy. Racial practices were institutionalized within American government, laws, and society.

9. **Race isn't biological, but racism is still real.** Race is a powerful social idea that gives people different access to opportunities and resources. Our government and social institutions have created advantages that disproportionately channel wealth, power, and resources to white people. This affects everyone, whether we are aware of it or not.

10. **Colorblindness will not end racism.** Pretending race doesn't exist is not the same as creating equality. Race is more than stereotypes and individual prejudice. To combat racism, we need to identify and remedy social policies and institutional practices that advantage some groups at the expense of others.

RACE - The Power of an Illusion was produced by California Newsreel in association with the Independent Television Service (ITVS). Major funding provided by the Ford Foundation and the Corporation for Public Broadcasting Diversity Fund. https://www.pbs.org/race/000_About/002_04-background-01-x.htm

Business Case for Diversity & Inclusion: A Chamber of Commerce Commitment

THE EAU CLAIRE Chamber of Commerce, Wisconsin, set up a task force to commit to the diversity and inclusion gap in the city. The author was part of the committee and wants to share this commitment.

Task Force Goal Statement

To share information and learn best practices about diversity, inclusion and minority business development to improve our workforce.

- The Committee discussed many articles about the state of chief diversity officers in the workforce.
    - A major issue the Committee identified relates to the fact that only 17% of the diversity officers in America have a business background. Instead, most have either human resources or legal experience. This, the Committee agreed, is an issue because diversity and inclusion must be tied directly to business-oriented results to have the most

success for and highest impact on organizations. When human resources employees lead diversity-and-inclusion efforts, recruitment initiatives produce the results that will get executives and other branches of the organization to buy into the efforts.
- Another common trend the Committee observed is this: many businesses will pull their top sales people out of the sales department and have them lead recruitment efforts. While this is positive in many respects, it carries risks. For one, that tactic could indirectly perpetuate diversity-related issues because those people might not be sufficiently trained in diversity-improvement skills.

Characteristics of a successful diversity and inclusion director:

- Wesley Escondo, chair of the committee drew the Committee's attention to an article, this one identifying the characteristics of a successful diversity and inclusion director. The members distilled the traits down to this: a successful director knows how to talk to many different people—people of all colors, sexualities, religions, etc.—and share the goals of the effort in a way that will maximize involvement.
- The committee challenged themselves to think of people they know can effectively do those things.

Internal diversity and inclusion surveys:

- Research shows that 60 percent of diversity-and-inclusion directors conduct internal surveys, but only 28 percent of them think that they are helpful in their efforts. The committee discussed reasons for why that number might be so low. One member remarked that surveys are imprecise measurements of overall trends and programs because many people fill them out based on how they feel about their job on the day that they fill them out.

- A committee member, Vicki, summarized her recent interview (2018) with Nestle, who has overall strategic plans but leaves implementation up to local plants. There was continued discussion of how to share best practices and other knowledge, such as a website with clickable links. There was also continued discussion of the idea of a D&I award. Further dialogue was needed regarding what the committee would want to recognize, its criteria, and the best venue at which to give it.

The Committee's Definition of Diversity and Inclusion is below:

- Diversity in the workforce means respecting and appreciating differences in, for example, race, culture, ethnicity, nationality, gender, gender expression, sexual orientation, age, national origin, people with a disability, religion, veteran status, class, and education.
- Inclusion is about focusing on the needs of every individual and ensuring the right conditions are in place for each person to achieve his/her full potential.

Survey to the Workforce.

The survey below was finalized and sent to the workforce to sample opinions of workforce diversity and inclusion. Your organization can adopt this best practice survey.

1. Number of employees in your company/organization?
   - ☐ 1-10
   - ☐ 11-49
   - ☐ 50-99
   - ☐ 100-249
   - ☐ 250-499
   - ☐ 500+

2. What is your organization's industry classification?
   - ☐ Accommodation & Food Services
   - ☐ Agriculture, Forestry, Fishing & Hunting
   - ☐ Arts, Entertainment & Recreation
   - ☐ Construction
   - ☐ Educational Services
   - ☐ Finance, Insurance, Real Estate
   - ☐ Healthcare & Social Assistance
   - ☐ Manufacturing
   - ☐ Professional, Scientific & Technical Services
   - ☐ Public Administration
   - ☐ Transportation, Communications, Electric, Gas, Sanitary Services
   - ☐ Wholesale Trade
   - ☐ Retail Trade
   - ☐ Other

3. Does your company have a Diversity & Inclusion program or department?
   - ☐ Yes
     - ➢ How effective is the program or department?
       - ☐ Very effective
       - ☐ Somewhat effective
       - ☐ Not very effective
       - ☐ Unknown effect
       - ☐ Too early to tell

   - ☐ No

➤ What barriers have prevented your company from establishing a D & I program or department?
  ☐ Cost
  ☐ Time/resources to implement/run the program
  ☐ Insufficient support from owner(s)/management
  ☐ Need more education
  ☐ Unsure about starting sensitive conversations
  ☐ Unsure how to recruit diverse talent
  ☐ Past negative experiences
  ☐ Would like to do something at our location, but decisions are controlled by a remotely located central office
  ☐ Other

☐ I don't know

4. Does your organization actively recruit employees from a diverse population?
   ☐ Yes
   o How do you actively recruit diverse applicants? Check all that apply:
     ☐ Postings at job service or workforce employment center
     ☐ Contacting college and university career centers
     ☐ Partnerships with diversity related advocacy organizations
     ☐ Postings at diversity-related publications or websites
     ☐ Postings or tables at diversity - related job fairs
     ☐ Postings at Department of Vocational Rehabilitation
     ☐ Establishing summer internship and mentoring programs
     ☐ Postings at Independent Living Centers
     ☐ Other (Include space to write in other info)
   ☐ No
   o Why doesn't your company recruit employees from a diverse population?
   ☐ I don't know

5. My company promotes Diversity & Inclusion through its:
   • Recruitment practices
     ☐ Strongly Agree
     ☐ Agree
     ☐ Neither Agree nor Disagree
     ☐ Disagree
     ☐ Strongly Disagree

- Hiring Practices
    - ☐ Strongly Agree
    - ☐ Agree
    - ☐ Neither Agree nor Disagree
    - ☐ Disagree
    - ☐ Strongly Disagree
- Employee Professional Development
    - ☐ Strongly Agree
    - ☐ Agree
    - ☐ Neither Agree nor Disagree
    - ☐ Disagree
    - ☐ Strongly Disagree
- Promotion Practices
    - ☐ Strongly Agree
    - ☐ Agree
    - ☐ Neither Agree nor Disagree
    - ☐ Disagree
    - ☐ Strongly Disagree
- Retention Strategies
    - ☐ Strongly Agree
    - ☐ Agree
    - ☐ Neither Agree nor Disagree
    - ☐ Disagree
    - ☐ Strongly Disagree

6. Do you perceive that your company/organization serve a diverse clientele?
    - ☐ Yes
        - o If so, what types of clientele?
            - ☐ Races, ethnicities and/or nationalities
            - ☐ Genders
            - ☐ Gender expressions and/or sexual orientations
            - ☐ Ages
            - ☐ Disabilities
            - ☐ Religions
            - ☐ Veteran status
            - ☐ Other: _____
    - ☐ No

7. Check all options below that your company has done to support Diversity & Inclusion in the past 12 months?
    - ☐ Published a blog post on D & I
    - ☐ Distributed an all-staff communication regarding D & I

- ☐ Created a D & I committee/task force/unit/program
- ☐ Supported staff to organize a company/organization sponsored D & I event or council
- ☐ Attended an event focusing on D & I
- ☐ Offered professional development opportunities related to D & I
- ☐ Created an Employee Resource Group
- ☐ Other: _____

8. What percentage of the leadership team in your company/organization is made up of diverse individuals?
   - ☐ 0%
   - ☐ 1% - 25%
   - ☐ 26% - 50%
   - ☐ 51% - 75%
   - ☐ 76% - 100%
   - ☐ I don't know

9. My company does the following:
   - Regularly evaluates its facilities/operations for disability access (e.g. physical access, restroom accommodations for transgender individuals, accessibility for individuals with limited sight, hearing).
       - ☐ Strongly Agree
       - ☐ Agree
       - ☐ Neither Agree nor Disagree
       - ☐ Disagree
       - ☐ Strongly Disagree
   - Provides workplace accommodations for employees with disabilities to facilitate performance.
       - ☐ Strongly Agree
       - ☐ Agree
       - ☐ Neither Agree nor Disagree
       - ☐ Disagree
       - ☐ Strongly Disagree
   - Uses images representing diverse populations for advertisements, collateral material and external communications.
       - ☐ Strongly Agree
       - ☐ Agree
       - ☐ Neither Agree nor Disagree
       - ☐ Disagree
       - ☐ Strongly Disagree
   - Enforces internal policies to provide equity and support for diverse employees, including advocacy beyond affirmative action, Equal Opportunity, and Americans with Disabilities Act requirements.
       - ☐ Strongly Agree

- ☐ Agree
- ☐ Neither Agree nor Disagree
- ☐ Disagree
- ☐ Strongly Disagree
• Retention Strategies
    - ☐ Strongly Agree
    - ☐ Agree
    - ☐ Neither Agree nor Disagree
    - ☐ Disagree
    - ☐ Strongly Disagree

Please check all areas your organization is interested in learning more about.
- ☐ Unconscious / Implicit Bias
- ☐ How to find diverse individuals in my area of business
- ☐ Reasonable accommodations and workers compensation
- ☐ Inclusion and safety in the workplace
- ☐ How to facilitate conversations regarding diversity and inclusion
- ☐ Diversity and discipline
- ☐ Working with Division of Vocational Rehabilitation
- ☐ Litigation Concerns

Final Ideation: My Message to You.

My Message to You:

The workplace has become a moving target. Just when you think you have things figured out, they are likely to change on you. To increase your chances of success, try to develop the skills and characteristics indicated below:

1. Learn to handle change. Welcome it and make it work for you.
2. Develop a "future" of orientation. Decide what kind of future you want to create for yourself beyond today or even this year.
3. Question existing assumptions, models and paradigms. Continually ask how things might be better.
4. Develop a wide array of skills to handle variety of jobs and work duties. Variety is becoming the norm, and people who can do many things are in demand.
5. Understand what it means to be a participant in a global economy.
6. Develop a wide scale of communication skills and become an expert in interpersonal relations.
7. Become an expert decision maker, problem solver and critical thinker.
8. Develop the creativity and confidence necessary to become an entrepreneur, innovator and risk taker.

9. Be a life-long learner. Don't ever talk about "finishing my education."
10. Develop sensitivity in working with people representing a wide variety of values, attitudes, languages, cultures, and beliefs. Understand the social, ethical and economic contexts of work.
11. Become technologically literate. This does not mean becoming an expert. It means developing a comfort level with technology.
12. Learn how institutions operate. You will be part of an institution or organization for much of your life. Be aware of how it works.
13. Develop an understanding of how you fit into the larger picture. You probably will not be working in isolation. It is important for you to know your work is related to others in the organization.
14. Learn to negotiate. Frequent change often means conflict. Being able to work it out will be a very important skill.
15. Learn how to work cooperatively in groups.
16. Develop the ability to articulate a point of view and to hear and deal with opposing points of view.
17. Develop a value system and observe how your actions are affected by your values.
18. Learn how to ask the right questions to get at the heart of a problem.
19. Develop a good relationship with yourself. This must occur before you can develop good relationships with others.

"Information without Application Leads to Frustration" – Larry Burkett.

We begin with a story:

The Goose Story.

Next fall, when you see geese heading south for the winter – flying along in *V* formation – you might consider what science has discovered as to why they fly that way. As each bird flaps its wings, it creates an uplift for the bird immediately following. By flying in *V* formation, the whole flock adds at least 71% greater flying range than if each bird flew on its own.

People who share a common direction (as in leadership and followership) and sense of community can get to where they are going more quickly and easily because they are traveling on the trust of one another.

When a goose falls out of formation, it suddenly feels the drag and resistance of trying to go it alone – and quickly gets back into formation to take advantage of the lifting power of the bird in front. If we have as much sense as a goose, we will stay in formation with those who are headed the same way we are.

When the Head Goose gets tired, it rotates back in the wing and another goose fly point. It is sensible to take turns doing demanding jobs or leading people as geese do flying south.

Geese honk from behind to encourage those upfront to keep up their speed. What do we say when we honk from behind?

Finally, and this is important – when a goose gets sick, or is wounded by gunshots, and falls out of formation, two other geese fall out with that goose and follow it down to lend help and protection. They stay with the fallen goose until it is able to fly, or until it dies; only then do they launch out on their own or with another formation to catch up with their group.

If we have the sense of the goose, we will stand by each other like that!

> *Angeles Arrien, based on work of Milton Olson.*

2017 Statistics of What Business Owners say They Want Most in New Employees.

Dependability	35%
Honesty	27%
Competency	19%
Good Attitude	19%

Source: Pacific Institute, Thought Patterns for Successful Career.

My Vision:

I want you to have a vision. For the vision exercise, please do the following:

a. Name: _____

b. The reasons I am going to school are_____
_____
_____

c. I want my life to look like this when I finish school ____
_____
_____
_____

Create A Future

a. What is your goal in life or what do you want to do in life to change your world? _____
_____
_____
_____
_____
_____

Vision:

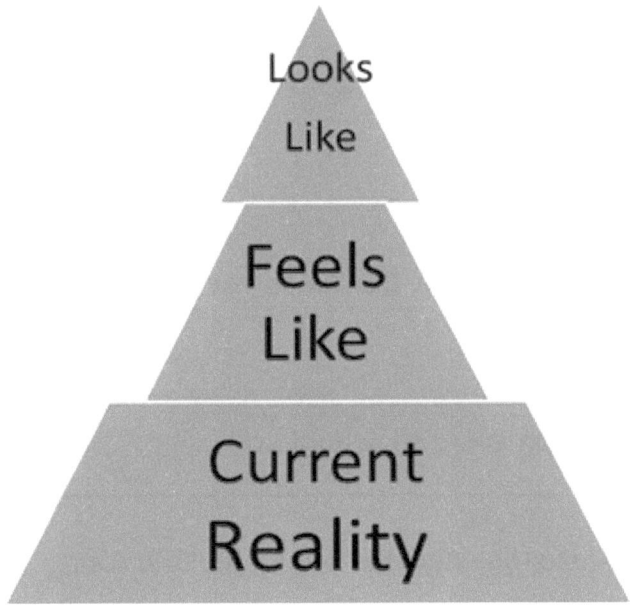

Use this pyramid to help you move towards your vision. Identify what the problem is (current reality) and would it be without the problem (vision). What words describe what it looks like to achieve your vision? What words describe how it feels to achieve your vision? List these words under each heading:

Looks Like: _____
_____

Feels Like: _____
_____

Current Reality: _____
_____

Plan S.M.A.R.T
S. Specific
M. Measurable
A. Action/Agreed to
R. Realistic
T. Time Specific

And Hit the Bull's Eye

Unleashing Your Potential

Potential (Can Do) ➡ Habits
　　　　　　　　　　Attitudes
　　　　　　　　　　Beliefs
　　　　　　　　　　Expectations

➡ Achievement (Actually Do)

a. State two potentials you have_____
_____
_____

b. Summarize your Habits /Attitudes/Beliefs/ ExpectationHabits/Attitudes/Beliefs/Expectations
_____
_____
_____

c. What do you hope to achieve in college based on your Potentials and Habits/Attitudes/Beliefs/Expectations?
_____
_____
_____
_____

Affirmations

Now boldly affirm what you will do as a habit.

In order to make a change in ourselves, we need to read our affirmations at least twice a day, for several weeks. There is something even more powerful at work in us. A vow –a one-time affirmation – made with great emotion can change your life forever.

Affirmations consist of action words or a vow that is accurate, realistic and elicit emotions to the individual.

Sample of Affirmation:

I <u>thrive</u> on my <u>daily</u> <u>jogging</u> program because it makes me feel <u>healthy</u>, <u>strong</u> and <u>energetic.</u>

Thrive – Action
Daily – Accurate
Jogging – Realistic
Healthy, strong, energetic – Emotional

Other examples of Affirmations:

    a. Taking tests is easy for me because I study and prepare for them well in advance.
    b. Because of my careful advance planning, I am well rested for my exams.
    c. I am healthy and energetic because I treat my body with the love and respect I deserve.
    d. I sincerely care about my professors and I am open-minded about what they teach me.

Now, write five affirmations of your own:

a._____

b._____

c._____

d._____

e. _____

Additional Exercise:

Write an affirmation for each of the following situations as if you were with the problem. Recognize that the person with the problem wants to change.

Problem: Denise feels she is too old to be in school, but wants an education.

> **Solution**:
>
> **Affirmation**:

Problem: Jane has ongoing child care problems she would like to be able to solve

> **Solution**:
>
> **Affirmation**:

Problem: Ken has been concerned about his student loan. He feels very frustrated and worried.

> **Solution**:
>
> **Affirmation**:

Attaining Our Best Futures:

Now, familiarize yourself with these learning principles to attain your best future:

Up until today, many of us have let a fear of new things, new places or new people keep us from moving toward the futures we want for ourselves and our families. No more. Throughout this semester, we will gain the knowledge and learn the tools and techniques that will help us attain our best futures.

1. **What is Holding Me Back?**
   The question we must all ask ourselves is, "Am I seeing all there is to see?" Most of us don't realize that we don't see everything because of the way we were raised, where we were raised and how we were taught. Exactly so because culture influences education in different locations. The good news is that we can see more than we've seen in the past, and this will open up a new future for each of us.

2. **Who Am I Listening To?**
   Most of us have spent our lives listening to others tell us "the way it is," and we believed them. What we didn't do was to question if what they said was the truth or an opinion. We must learn to become skeptical listeners.

3. **Lock-On/Lock-Out**
   Each of us have tremendous potential, and no one can know its limits. For the most part, we are only limited by our beliefs, our truths, and sometimes, the absence of the truth will set us free.

4. **My Brains Filter System.**
   The human brain has a formation in the central cortex, the reticular activating system (RAS), which filters all the information that is bombarding our senses. It only lets through that which is important to us right now. We can put the RAS to work for us, by setting clear, concise goals, so that the right information gets through to us.

5. **How My Mind Works.**
   As scientists unravel the mysteries of the human brain, the magnificent complexity of its structure, we have discovered

the levels of the mind involved in the thought-process. Our conscious, subconscious and creative subconscious work together to perceive the world around us, store our reality and make sure that each of us acts like the person we know ourselves to be.

6. **Free Flowing at a New Level.**
   As we dig deeper into our thought-processes, we see that we are constantly taking our perceptions of current reality and checking them against our past stored reality in our subconscious. We need to remember that this stored reality isn't just a memory of what has happened, but our feelings about what has happened to us.

7. **Learning in the Right Direction.**
   There is a great advantage to being able to rely on our habits. We don't need to stop and think about how to do many routine things. However, when those habits keep us stuck in a rut, underliving our potential, we need to see about changing them. In the same manner, our attitudes can limit our achievements. The good news is that habits and attitudes can changed.

8. **How My Beliefs are Formed.**
   Our thoughts accumulate to become beliefs, so it is important to control our thoughts. We do this by controlling our self-talk, that constant conversation that goes on in our minds. This self-talk is vitally important in forming our self-image, and can either build us up or tear us down. In fact, understanding the power of self-talk may be the most important thing we can ever learn.

9. **Building My Self-Image.**
   The subconscious mind is a literal mechanism. It does what you tell it. If with your self-talk, you are dwelling on the negative that is what gets assimilated into your version of

"reality" in the subconscious. Since thoughts accumulate to become beliefs, all of your beliefs become negative, and reaching your potential will not be possible. Now, if your self-talk dwells on the positive possibilities of life, what will happen to your beliefs and your behavior?

10. **My Future is Up To Me**
Human beings are picture oriented. What we dwell on in our minds tends to come about in our lives. So, it is important to dwell on what we do want, and use our self-talk to see ourselves into the future – the future we want.

11. **I am Worth It.**
Giving sanctions, or agreeing with what others say to us about ourselves is risky business. What we are really agreeing with are the opinions of others, and they may not be the truth. Then, we use our self-talk to reinforce a bad opinion, and before we know it, we tear down our sense of self-esteem. We need to remember our successes, and assimilate them fully, so that we escalate our self-worth, our self-esteem.

12. **Make the Unfamiliar Familiar**
In our past, when we really didn't want to go somewhere or do something, we found excellent reasons for not going or doing. What we may not have realized is that we were coming face-to-face with our comfort zones. While some comfort zones are good for us, others hold us back; and it is time that we learn how to expand those limiting comfort zones and allow ourselves to grow.

13. **Putting Life on a Want-To**
We have all felt, at one time or another, like we were being forced into doing something against our will. We may have done it, but we rebelled every step of the way. We felt pushed and we pushed back and it used up a lot

of energy while it made us feel unhappy. What if we put life on a "want-to" basis, and used all that energy and creativity toward making a happy life for ourselves and those around us.

14. **Making the Pictures Match.**
When the world outside doesn't match the pictures of the world we hold in our minds, we have a problem. The creative subconscious goes to work to make the pictures match. We get lots of energy, and we get very creative. This is human nature. However, we can take hold of this process and use it to help us make the positive changes we want in our lives, using our power of visualization to reach our goals.

15. **I Can See It!**
It is a fact of life – literally – human beings need goals. If we have no goals, we die. Since the survival instinct is so strong, if we have no new goals, we simply recreate our old ones and life doesn't change very much. We must dream big and give ourselves goals, causing tremendous energy and creativity inside ourselves to achieve these goals.

16. **My Better Future**
It is normal for us to want to know "how" we are going to get where we want to go. But, we really don't need to know the "how" in order to set or goals. In fact, if we demand to know "how" first, we will usually back up our goals to match our current abilities, and we don't grow very much.

17. **My Goals – My Vision – My Future**
We know the importance of setting goals and how to visualize what we want for our lives. Now it is time to learn how to write out our goals effectively for the maximum positive impact on our futures. Know how to write your goals.

18. **If I Want It, I Can Create It.**
    By growing stronger on the inside, we allow ourselves to dream bigger and set bigger goals. In order to grow stronger on the inside, we need to escalate our self-efficacy – our belief in our own ability to make things happen in our lives. We look forward to success, and not fear of failure; and if we don't reach or goals, we are resilient. We pick ourselves up, and start again.

19. **Rites of Passage**
    In order to make a change in ourselves, we need to read our affirmations at least twice a day, for several weeks. A vow –a one-time affirmation – made with great emotion can change your life forever. Rites of passage do the same… it changes our lives for the better.

REFERENCES

Abrams, R. (2010). *Hire Your First Employee*. Palo Alto, CA: The Planning Shop.

Bem, D.J., (1970). *Attitude and human affair*. Belmont, CA: Brooks Cole.

Carnevales, A.P. and Rose, S.J. (2003). Socioeconomic status, race/ethnicity, and selective college admissions (A Century Foundation Paper). New York, NY: The Century Foundation.

Chaiken, A.L., & Derlega, V.J., (1976). *Self-disclosure*. Morristown, NJ: General Learning Press.

Clary, A. (21 July, 2015). Coaching and Mentoring. YouTube link https://www.youtube.com/watch?v=tWaNC1jvaIY

Covey, S. R. (2004). *The 7 Habits of Highly Effective People*. New York, NY: Simon & Chuster.

Diversity. Excerpted from The Art of Mindful Facilitation by Lee Mun Wah (2004). Stirfry Seminars & Consulting (510) 204-8840 / www.stirryseminars.com

Every Manager's Desk Reference (2002). Conflict Resolution. Penguin Publishing Group. ALPHA Publication.

Forbes Nine traits of grant writing. Retrieved from https://www.forbes.com/sites/forbesnonprofitcouncil/2018/05/29/nine-traits-of-effective-grant-writers-who-write-great-proposals/#35a804955d8b

Gardner, W. L., Avolio, B.J., Luthans, F., May, D.R., & Walumba, F. (2005). *Can you see the real me?* A self-based model of authentic leader and follower development. *Leadership Quarterly, 16*, 343-372.

Gladieux, E., (2004). *Low-income students and the affordability of higher education.* In R.D. Kehlenberg (Ed.), America's untapped resource: Low-income students in higher education. New York: The Century Foundation Press.

Greenleaf, R. K. (1991). **The Servant Leader.** Westfield, IN: The Robert Greenleaf Center.

Greenleaf, R. K. (1998). **The Power of Servant Leadership.** San Francisco, CA: Berrett-Koehler.

Heifetz, R.A., & Linsky, M. (2002). *Leadership on the line: Staying alive through the dangers of leading.* Boston: Harvard Business Press.

Highhouse, S. (2002). Judgment and decision-making research: Relevance to industrial and organizational psychology. In N. Anderson, D. S. Ones, H. K. Sinangil, & C. Viswesvaran (Eds.), **Handbook of industrial, work and organizational** *psychology, Vol. 2. Organizational psychology* (pp. 314-331). Thousand Oaks, CA, US: Sage Publications, Inc.

Isaacs, W., (1999). *Dialogue and the art of thinking together.* New York: Currency and Doubleday.

Katz, D., & Stotland, E. (1959). *A preliminary statement to a theory of structure and change.* New York: McGraw-Hill.

Katz, L. (2006). *Negotiating International Business.* Charleston, SC: Booksurge.

Kluckhohn, F.R., & Strodtbeck, F.L., (1976). *Variations in value orientations.* Westport, Conn: Greenwood Press Publishers.

Leadership Through Stewardship. Retrieved from https://nytimesineducation.com/spotlight/leadership-through-stewardship-a-foundation-for-organizational-success-across-cultures/.

Light, A., and Strayer, W. (2000). Determinants of college completion: School quality of student ability? *Journal of Human Resources, 35* (2) 299-332

Maple, S.A., & Stage, F.K. (1991). Influences on the choices of math/science major by gender and ethnicity. *American Educational Research Journal, 28*(1). 37-60

Matsumoto (1998). Emotions and Intercultural Communication. *International Communications Research, 11,* 1-32

Matsumoto (2003). *The robustness of Intercultural Adjustments Potential Scale* (ICAPS): *The search for universal psychological engine of adjustment. International Journal of Intercultural Relations, 27*(5), 543-562

Osgood, C.E. (1962). *The principle of congruity is the predisposition of attitude change.* New York: McGraw-Hill

Osgood, C.E., (1962). *The measurement of meaning.* Urbana: University of Illinois Press.

Rask, K., & Tiefenthaler, J. (2008). The role of grade sensitivity in explaining gender imbalance in undergraduate economics. *Economics of Education Review, 12,* 1-8

Rodin, R. S. (2010). *The steward leader: Transforming people, organizations, and communities.* Madison, WI: InterVarsity Press.

Schein, E.H., (1992). *Organizational culture and leadership.* 2nd Edition, San Francisco: Jossey-Bass, 17.

Spears, L. C. (1995). **Reflections and Leadership**. New York: John Wiley and Sons.

Spears, L. C. (2002). Character and Servant Leadership: Ten Characteristics of Effective and Caring Leaders. **Journal of Virtues and Leadership, 1**(1), 25-30.

Steward Leadership. Retrieved from http://nytimesineducation.com/spotlight/what-is-stewardship-and-should-all-great-leaders-practice-it/

Steward Leadership: IEDP https://www.iedp.com/articles/steward-leadership/.

The 10 best practices of diversity. Retrieved from https://diversityofficermagazine.com/diversity-inclusion/top-ten-diversity-best-practices/

USA Today/The Associated Press (2009). Multicultural education. Implications for curriculum design. March 5, 2009.

Van Velsor, E., McCauley, D.D., & Ruderman, M.N. (Eds.). (2010). *Handbook of leadership Development*. San Francisco: Jossey-Bass.

Vu, M. A. (2011). Rick Warren, Tony Blair Talk about Faith, Mideast, 9/11. *The Christian Post* [quoted from *Civil Forum on Peace in a Globalized Economy*, Saddleback Church, March 6, 2011]

What is Steward Leadership? Design Group International. Retrieved from https://www.designgroupinternational.com/blogs/sustainable-vision-with-matthew-thomas/what-is-stewardship-steward-leadership.

Williams, C. (2018). MGMT: Principles of Management (11th ed.). Boston, MA: Cengage.

Williams, C. (2019). *Principles of Management.* (11th ed.). Boston, MA: Cengage.

Wirt S., Kincheloe, J.L., and Steinberg, S.R. (2004). *The Condition of Education 2004* (NCES 2004-077). U.S Department of Education, National Center for Education Statistics. Washington, DC: U.S. Government Printing Office.

Zanna. M.P., & Rampel, J.K. (1988). *Attitude. A New Look At An Old Concept*. New York: Cambridge University Press.

www.ingramcontent.com/pod-product-compliance
Lightning Source LLC
LaVergne TN
LVHW040141080526
838202LV00042B/2987